Water Infrastructure
Equitable Deployment of Resilient Systems

Water
Infrastructure

Equitable Deployment of Resilient Systems

S. Bry Sarté and Morana M. Stipisic
Foreword by Kate Orff

CONTENTS

TECHNOLOGY

 1

 2

 3

 4

ECOLOGY

 5

 6

FINANCE

EQUITY

FOREWORD

What is next-century urban design? What tools will urban designers need, and what design methodologies will they explore? Increasingly, the urban designer synthesizes modes of working from many fields: architecture, landscape, engineering, politics, and sociology, to name a few. Urban design practice itself serves as a form of connective infrastructure, bridging segregated disciplinary thought to meet the complex challenges posed by urbanization.

At the same time, modern infrastructure typologies that were largely centralized, hidden, waste-generating, and monofunctional are being replaced by more widely dispersed and aggregated forms that integrate waste processes and, moreover, are embedded in communities. This has profound implications for urban design, for systems maintenance, and for social life.

Urban Innovations is a groundbreaking series by the Columbia Urban Design Program on next-century infrastructure. In this series, we aim to explore both how the practice of urban design bridges and connects forms of knowledge, and how physical infrastructure has shaped and will continue to shape the ongoing process of urbanization.

The first book in the series, *Water Infrastructure,* tackles the issue of water and sanitation as one of the most pressing and urgent issues of our time in a global context. S. Bry Sarté and Morana M. Stipisic highlight the ways in which resilient design for water infrastructure can be reframed as critical connective tissue and as a living system that provides a variety of benefits such as decreasing urban heat island effects, releasing pressure on aging infrastructure, absorbing water for flood protection, filtering water and reuse, and providing ecological habitat and ecosystem services. In so doing, they give particular attention to challenges in the developing world, and the ways that strategies developed in cities in both the Global North and Global South may offer innovative solutions to the issues coastal cities everywhere are facing. Developed in part for the United Nations Habitat III conference, their succinct analysis is paired with helpful examples that can be useful to urban designers and planners, engineers, municipal agencies, and others concerned with creating a healthier and more inclusive urban environment. It examines how physical infrastructure itself is becoming multiform and multi-purpose, serving engineering, social, spatial, environmental and health benefits simultaneously. Fittingly, it is designed as a tool kit to enable change on a broader, global scale, and to address water and urban design as one of the central issues of our time with clarity and purpose.

—Kate Orff

ACKNOWLEDGEMENTS

Special thanks to

Josiah Cain
Prentiss Darden
Angela Eaton

Grimshaw Architects
Columbia University School of Architecture, Planning, and Preservation
Huairou Commission
The Municipal Arts Society
Urban Design Lab, Columbia University's Earth Institute
Urban Design Program at GSAPP

Bina Bhatia
Yureeah Kim
Michael Maloney
Jun Park
Isha Patel
Manuela Powidayko Alberici Souza
Yuda Sun
Nour Zoghby
Ashwini Karanth
Juliana Azem Ribeiro de Almeida
Juan Guzmán-Palacios

Design by

Manuel Miranda Practice

Produced with generous support of

Sherwood Institute and
Sherwood Design Engineers

This publication is officially supported by the preparatory process for United Nations bi-decennial Conference on Housing and Sustainable Urban Development Habitat III to take place in October 2016 in Quito, Ecuador. The launch is planned to take place during the Third Preparatory Commission for Habitat III on July 25, 2016 in Surabaya, Indonesia. Intention of this publication is to present work in progress and stimulate constructive conversation. As a part of the Habitat III preparatory process it is aiming to contribute a concrete set of recommendations related to resilient urban water infrastructure to the New Urban Agenda.

The authors of this publication representing Sherwood Institute and Columbia University's Urban Design Lab took the initiative to host the forum Innovations in Urban Infrastructure: Where Policy Meets Practice on

September 15–16 of 2014. The aim of this effort was to respond to the request made by Dr. Joan Clos, the Executive Director of United Nations Human Settlements Programme (UN-Habitat), and propose a set of concrete recommendations for design and planning of urban environments. The Forum gathered individuals from academia, government, business, United Nations community and women's organizations, representatives from the field of architecture, engineering, landscape, urban design, planning, and related fields. During two active days of workshops those experts generated recommendations for the Habitat III preparatory process.

The Forum was officially recognized as a Habitat III Preparatory Commission 1 Parallel Event. The findings from the Forum were shared at the side event "Resilient Cities at the Intersection of Social and Physical Infrastructure" hosted by Sherwood Institute, Columbia University, and Municipal Art Society. This side event was officially recognized and took place at the UN Headquarters in New York City. Following the Forum and Side Event, Sherwood Institute hosted a workshop at the San Francisco Verge conference in October 2014 to get direct review from the business technology sector. Over the next six months the authors continued to advance the summary of the publication in collaboration with Earth Institute's Urban Design Lab, community advisors, women's organizations, and design professionals located worldwide.

The published draft of the material was presented as an official side event of the Second Preparatory Commission (PC2) for Habitat III: The Urban Multiplier Effect: Community Building through Resilient and Inclusive Infrastructure. PC2 took place on April 14, 2015 in Nairobi, Kenya. It focused on social inclusiveness, generated much interest, and led to the production of a complete publication. One of the initiatives the authors took part in organizing jointly with the Municipal Art Society and The New School was the World Urban Campaign's Urban Thinkers Campus that took place in New York City on October 24, 2015. At this event a set of concrete policy-oriented recommendations were developed.

Columbia University's Graduate School of Architecture, Planning, and Preservation offers an Urban Design Seminar, Infrastructure, Resilience and Public Space, that the authors have been teaching for five years. Through work with graduate students the ideas were developed further and tested.

Instrumental in the whole process was the Habitat III Civil Society Working Group where the authors were active participants since the onset of the workings of this entity in the early Summer of 2014.

PART 1
Risks

This publication addresses water infrastructure vulnerability and risks associated with rapid urbanization and changing climate. It does so within the context of both formal and informal developments. In addition, it recommends particular innovations in water infrastructure systems and illustrates how to best implement those systems in order to achieve resilient, healthy, inclusive communities.

All The Water in the World

There is a finite amount of water in the world and an even more limited amount available to sustain our cities. This resource needs to be managed carefully. Depleted aquifers, contaminated surface waters, rising sea levels, increasing salinity in drinking water, desalination dependent on energy — these are the problems growing urban populations face related to water management.

Of all the water in the world, only 2.5 percent is freshwater, and only 0.3 percent is readily available for human consumption. This precious and finite resource is interwoven with water quality and availability risk in many of our cities.[1]

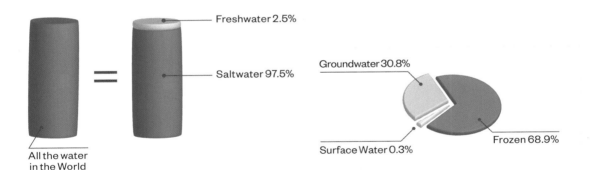

Varied Risks Ahead

Innovations associated with resilient infrastructure are becoming increasingly important as we face challenges and vulnerability due to increased population growth, urbanization, and the effects of climate change: sea level rise, changing precipitation patterns, increased storm frequency, and extreme temperatures. There are seven risks that affect the viability of many of our urban settlements.

RISK 1

 Informal settlements are often plagued by waterborne disease that proliferates in adjacent waters contaminated by untreated wastewater discharge. Children not only play and bathe in this water, but their families cook with it, use it for laundry and often, lacking better sources, drink it. This example is from Pasay City, on the outskirts of Manila.

 Central wastewater infrastructure, such as the Hyperion Wastewater Treatment Plant in Los Angeles above, provides needed treatment but does not always accomplish the required intent completely. Often central wastewater plants discharge nutrient-rich water to the receiving water bodies. Augmenting these systems can help to address the problem.

SANITATION & WATER POLLUTION

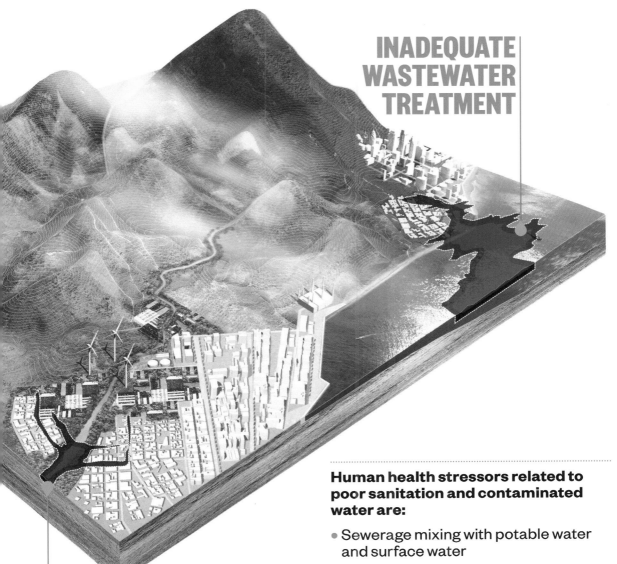

**INADEQUATE
WASTEWATER
TREATMENT**

**UNTREATED
SEWERAGE
RELEASE**

Human health stressors related to poor sanitation and contaminated water are:

- Sewerage mixing with potable water and surface water
- Health risks from polluted waters
- Erosion of coastal protections and ecosystems
- Over-extraction of freshwater sources
- Unsustainable land development
- Central wastewater plants may be inadequate to protect surface waters
- Landfill contamination of aquifers and surface waters
- E-waste polluting aquifers and surface water

RISK 2

Many cities are struggling to develop plans to respond effectively to the increasing risk of climate change induced coastal flooding. Havana, pictured, like many other coastal cities is bracing for coastal storms to increase in their intensity and frequency.

The eastern seaboard of the United States was struck by superstorm Sandy in 2012. This event helped to develop an increased sense of urgency in the US to tackle the growing challenges associated with coastal flood risk in a more comprehensive manner.

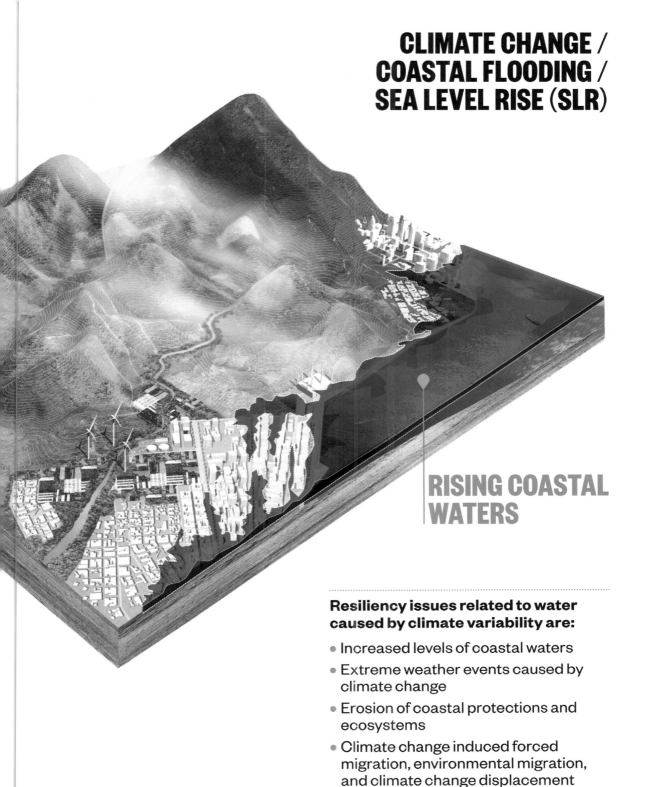

CLIMATE CHANGE /
COASTAL FLOODING /
SEA LEVEL RISE (SLR)

RISING COASTAL WATERS

Resiliency issues related to water caused by climate variability are:

- Increased levels of coastal waters
- Extreme weather events caused by climate change
- Erosion of coastal protections and ecosystems
- Climate change induced forced migration, environmental migration, and climate change displacement
- Disadvantaged populations at increased risk
- Increased salinity in coastal water supply

 Torrential rains create hazardous conditions in cities through extreme flooding, such as in Manila in 2012. Over $14 million in damages and losses resulted from the Manila floods.[2]

 Floods in Calgary, Canada during 2013, caused damage valued at $6 billion[3]. Losses due to flooding could cost $60-63 billion or more per year in major coastal cities in the United States by 2050[4].

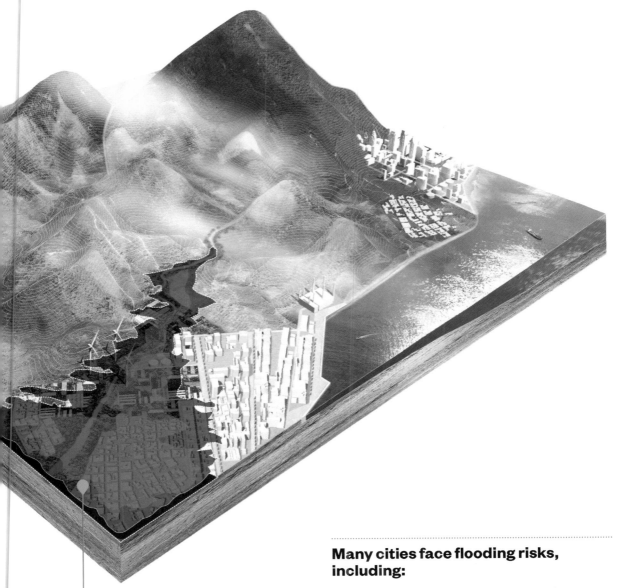

RIVERINE FLOODING

Many cities face flooding risks, including:

- Extreme weather events inducing flooding, storms, heat
- Poor water quality associated with urban runoff
- Unsustainable land development practices compounding flooding risks
- Habitat loss— and climate change displacement
- Spread of disease
- Erosion and loss of soil

Supply of water is an intense focus for many communities' survival. From traditional water scarce areas to major cities like Bangalore that face an uncertain future, the need for self-sufficient water supply is critical for community resilience.

Urban sprawl often rapidly expands into arid terrain unable to support the population density as pictured on the fringes of Lima.

Climate risks that affect urban water supply and increase water competition across both borders and use types are:

- Drought reducing surface and subsurface reserves
- Shift to energy-intensive water supplies
- Large water demands for thermal power plants (nuclear/fossil)
- Increased heat island effect due to lack of water/vegetation

RISK 5

 As utility construction practices vary around the globe so do the flaws that emerge in the decades after installation. While ruptured pipes create dramatic immediate challenges, continuously leaking pipes contribute to up to half of the efficiency losses in some municipal systems and an average of 15 percent in the US. Ailing and aging infrastructure can contribute to more than twenty billion gallons of water per year within a single municipality (Skokie, IL above).[5]

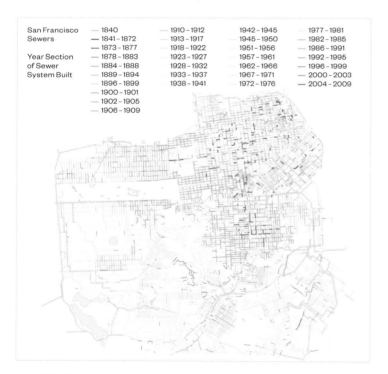

San Francisco Sewers	— 1840	— 1910 – 1912	1942 – 1945	— 1977 – 1981
	— 1841 – 1872	— 1913 – 1917	1945 – 1950	— 1982 – 1985
	— 1873 – 1877	— 1918 – 1922	1951 – 1956	— 1986 – 1991
Year Section	— 1878 – 1883	— 1923 – 1927	1957 – 1961	— 1992 – 1995
of Sewer	— 1884 – 1888	1928 – 1932	1962 – 1966	— 1996 – 1999
System Built	— 1889 – 1894	1933 – 1937	1967 – 1971	— 2000 – 2003
	— 1896 – 1899	1938 – 1941	1972 – 1976	— 2004 – 2009
	— 1900 – 1901			
	— 1902 – 1905			
	— 1906 – 1909			

 Evidence shows that sewer pipes over 100 years old are much more likely to fail than those less than 100 years old. In this diagram the sewer lines in red and orange are 100-150 years old, while lines in blue and green are newer. In many cities, the rate of repair is insufficient to prevent future crises.

FAILING / AGING INFRASTRUCTURE

UNADAPTABLE SYSTEMS

POLLUTING SYSTEMS

AGING INFRASTRUCTURE

INFRA-STRUCTURE VULNERABILITY

In the global north and south alike, aging infrastructure presents increasing risk:

- Infrastructure is aging and costly to repair
- Vulnerable to natural hazards and manmade disasters
- Cost / ability of large centralized systems to upgrade and respond to failure
- Systems often pollute the environment directly
- Centralized systems are expensive and slow to adapt

More than 1.8 million children under five years old die each year as a result of water related illness. Polluted water in Tamil Nadu, India pictured above.[6]

Twenty to fifty million tons of e-waste is generated worldwide annually, often being disposed of in a manner that pollutes waterways and water supplies. This example is from Guiyu, Guangdong Province, China.[7]

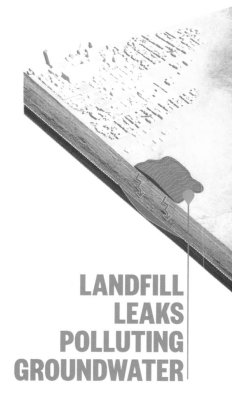

LANDFILL LEAKS POLLUTING GROUNDWATER

SOLID WASTE POLLUTING SURFACE WATER

Major water contamination results from unregulated disposal of:

- Household plastics
- Medical waste
- Industrial waste
- Electronic waste

RISK 7

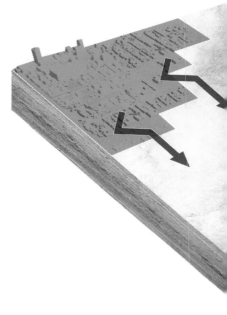

Urban areas often are completely paved creating minimal permeability of the soil resulting in accelerated runoff from rainfall events.

In addition to the pavement of roads for circulation, often stream channels are hardened resulting in a complete loss of the natural hydrological function and cleansing characteristics of undeveloped landscapes. Ballona Creek in Los Angeles is one such example.

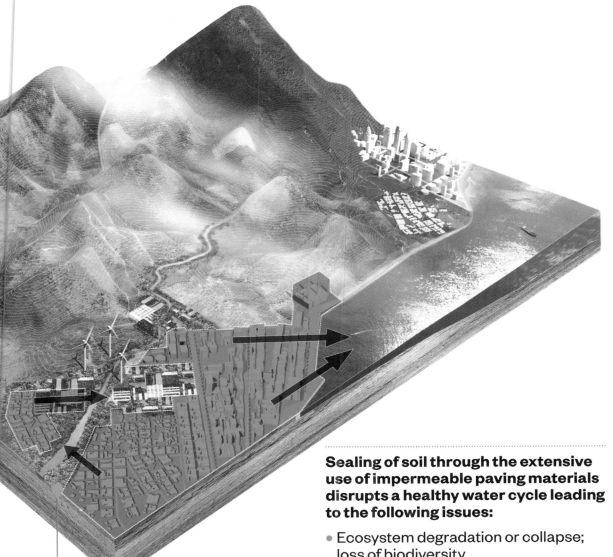

INCREASED PROBLEM OF STORMWATER RUNOFF

Sealing of soil through the extensive use of impermeable paving materials disrupts a healthy water cycle leading to the following issues:

- Ecosystem degradation or collapse; loss of biodiversity
- Human health impacts from air and water quality decline
- Preventing aquifer recharge
- Overloading existing stormwater infrastructure
- Speeding up the stormwater runoff resulting in the increase of its temperature
- The contribution to the creation of the heat island effect
- Loss of green public space

Speed of Urbanization

We are currently experiencing a period of rapid urbanization. According to the United Nations, the world population of 7.2 billion people is projected to increase by 2.5 billion people by 2050 with nearly 90 percent of the increase concentrated in urban areas of Asia and Africa. If new growth is not anticipated and planned for, it is likely that the result will be widespread informal settlements with poor access to basic services. This scale of unplanned urban growth could have devastating impacts on available resources, compromising access for large populations, and presenting potentially serious risks to human and ecological health.[8]

The world's population is experiencing an increased rate of growth and urbanization. Total urbanized land up to year 2000 is estimated at 252,000 square miles. Projections show total urbanized land may reach 720,000 square miles by 2030.[9]

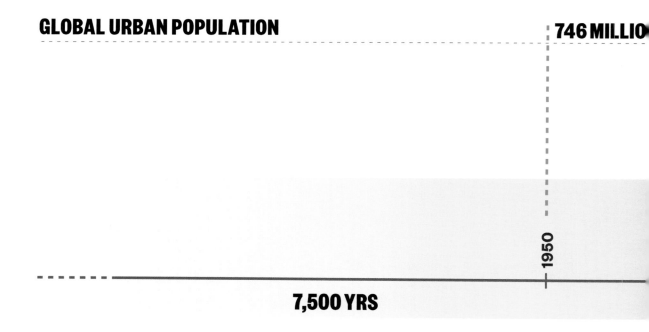

GLOBAL URBAN POPULATION

746 MILLIO

1950

7,500 YRS

First Cities   Urbanization

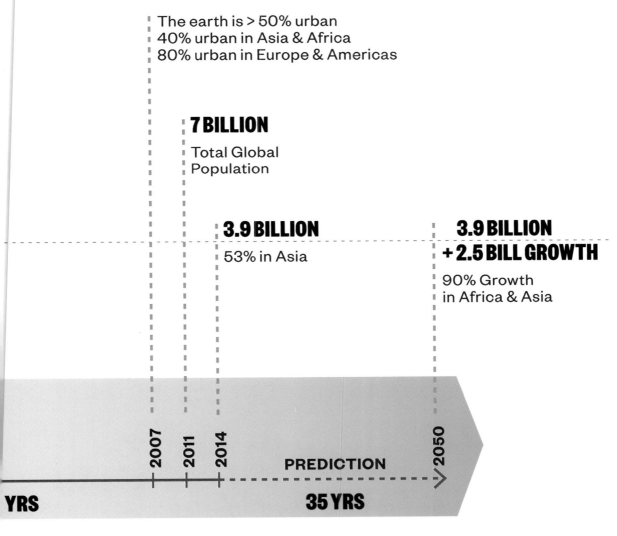

The earth is > 50% urban
40% urban in Asia & Africa
80% urban in Europe & Americas

7 BILLION

Total Global
Population

3.9 BILLION

53% in Asia

3.9 BILLION

+ 2.5 BILL GROWTH

90% Growth
in Africa & Asia

2007

2011

2014

2050

PREDICTION

YRS

35 YRS

Rapid Urbanization

Spontaneous Development

Projected population growth indicates an increasing urbanization trend. Globally, according to the UN, "more people live in urban areas than in rural areas, with 54 percent of the world's population residing in urban areas in 2014."[10] In addition, informal urban settlements are growing more rapidly than formal urban settlements in developing regions. UN-HABITAT indicated in 2001 that one third of the world's urban population, about 924 million people, live in slums. In developing regions, "slum dwellers account for 43 percent of the urban population, compared to 6 percent of the urban population in developed regions." This demographic, representing roughly one-sixth of humanity, resides in informal settlements lacking basic potable water and sanitation services.[11] Joan Clos, Executive Director of UN-HABITAT, reported in 2010 that despite "marked improvements for millions of slum-dwellers worldwide over the last decade, the number of people living in urban squalor was still rising and must be addressed through global action." To mitigate this trend, there is a need to focus on infrastructure prepared for an evolving future because infrastructure plays a critical role in urban design and the planning of healthy and inclusive cities. Access to clean water and proper wastewater treatment are vital to the health and safety of urban populations. Women and children living in informal settlements mostly lack these basic services.

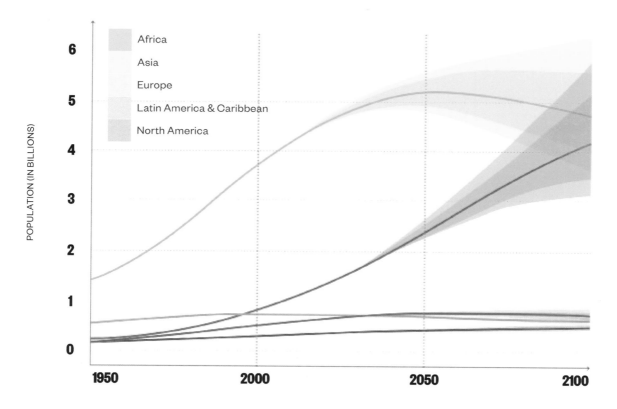

Population growth predictions relevant to geographical zones [12]

By 2030, about 60 percent of the world's population is expected to live in cities. As the number of urban dwellers increases, so does the number of slum dwellers. Estimated projections show nearly two billion people living in urban slums by 2030.[13]

Women & Water

Women have traditionally been the caretakers of families and communities, and they often possess substantial knowledge and organizational skills that can be used to improve the design, implementation, and maintenance of water infrastructure systems, particularly within the context of developing nations. Individual and collective needs for proper sanitation, a clean water supply, and financial independence are crucial elements needed for the success of women in our global society. Beyond improving daily living conditions, water infrastructure innovation can benefit women through job creation. Additionally, water infrastructure can be designed in a way to improve urban safety for women with well-lit public spaces and meeting points, perhaps powered by energy harnessed in wastewater treatment plants.

These solutions also give women opportunities to engage in fields like urban design, policy-making, and environmental health—industries that remain male-dominated. Women are particularly equipped to provide leadership in these roles because of the general capability and knowledge stemming from their being caretakers and heads in their community.

"Women from organized groups must be empowered with the capacity to participate in decision-making at all levels—from local community boards, to provincial assemblies, national governments, and at the United Nations."

—Huairou Commission

Aging Infrastructure

The need for innovations in water infrastructure is clear. In developed regions of the world, water infrastructure is aging and costly to repair. It was built during a time when sanitation and drainage were necessary for development, but has now reached the end of its lifecycle. Aging systems leak, fail, are vulnerable to natural hazards, and are costly to replace. Currently, centralized water infrastructure does not adapt easily to rapidly changing conditions related to population growth, urbanization, and climate change. In developing regions of the world, the lack of basic water and sanitation services needs to be addressed. Yet building the same centralized systems that developed regions are grappling with would be unsustainable. This presents an opportunity to implement evolved water infrastructure innovations that supply multiple benefits and are adaptable to changing conditions.

Ecological Health and Public Space

Ecological health supports human health. Advancing the role of productive and functioning ecological systems within our urban contexts will accelerate and help to restore the balance that must be advanced in the support of non-urban landscapes. Also of paramount importance is the role public space plays as a system that allows for the essential human interactions leading to social cohesion and stewardship of our cities. It is imperative to incorporate green infrastructure and high performance ecology into the urban fabric as it can sustain healthier communities, improve quality of life, and increase land value. The creation of ecologically functional public space as a tool of resilient development will contribute to climate change mitigation through urban heat island effect reduction and stimulation of a healthy water cycle while improving our habitat and the habitat of other species.

Innovation Needed

The challenges we face arise from rapid development of the built environment, which overtaxes natural systems and results in vulnerabilities and risks for human settlements. These vulnerabilities are multifaceted and need to be addressed from multiple perspectives to create comprehensive solutions for resilient communities. Water infrastructure systems provide the most basic life support. Equitable access to water can determine whether a developing city will succeed or fail. As global population increases, so, too, does the need to protect human settlements from fluctuations in climate and resources. Simply replicating the systems that were used in the past is not enough. A focus on public benefits that emerge from integrated and thoughtful water infrastructure strategies will change the way the cities of the future develop. New systems, sensitive to local contexts and cultures, should either complement or replace the centralized approach to water infrastructure. Innovating water infrastructure has the potential to address resiliency concerns in multiple ways that are mutually reinforcing. Through these lenses, the following infrastructure innovations and implementation strategies are an offering of tools that might be used by multiple stakeholder groups in the design, construction, and function of resilient communities.

PART 2

Design

Recomme

ndations

Infrastructure is a critical component of urban design that needs to be addressed to enable healthy and inclusive urban growth, especially in these times of rapid urbanization and changing weather patterns.

This publication aims to contribute a concrete set of recommendations related to resilient urban infrastructure with a particular focus on water, including sanitation, and its crossover with public space as a highly performative system.

These innovative and decentralized systems target formal and informal settlements in the developed and developing world alike. We are proposing its inclusion into the Habitat III action-oriented output document: the New Urban Agenda.

Cost of Infrastructure

The McKinsey Global Institute estimates that over $50 trillion will be needed globally to keep global economies growing at a moderate pace through 2030.[14] This investment needs to focus on both informal settlements that are struggling to provide basic sanitation and formal developments that increasingly face uncertain environmental and climate risks. Sick Water, a UN publication, states that, "According to the Green Economy Initiative, every dollar invested in safe water and sanitation has a pay back of $3 to $34, depending on the region and the technology deployed."[15]

2013 - 2030
$67 Trillion
Total Infrastructure Investment

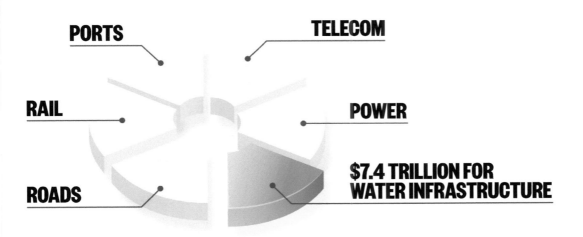

PORTS

TELECOM

RAIL

POWER

ROADS

$7.4 TRILLION FOR WATER INFRASTRUCTURE

To maintain a modest economic growth globally, $67 trillion needs to be invested between 2015 and 2035. This represents a tremendous opportunity to direct infrastructural investment in a manner that fosters not only economic progress but social and environmental as well.[16]

Formal and Informal Development

Formal and informal developments each present distinct challenges. Investments and strategies that prioritize interdependencies will enhance their mutual functions. In the context of these relationships, we have laid out a sequence of recommendations that address both of these development contexts.

Adaptable Systems

The innovations put forth in this publication represent progressive thinking in how we design infrastructure to be multifunctional, regenerative, and inclusive of various social groups. The innovations may change form when applied to informal settlements compared to formal settlements, but the concept remains intact. An important aspect of these innovations, particularly technology-focused innovations, is that they are adaptable to fluctuations in population and climatic conditions.

Multifunctional Infrastructure

New versions of infrastructure have the capacity to be multifunctional rather than monofunctional. Efficient infrastructure can simultaneously create safe water supplies, support ecology, and provide public spaces while bringing multiple benefits to urban dwellers and providing structure for more resilient cities. Key opportunities that offer chances for social inclusiveness, economic development, and disaster risk reduction should be sought. Infrastructure investments that can capitalize on linked resource flows that manage energy water and waste while sustaining ecological systems should be prioritized.

Closed Loops

A key component of developing successful water systems is finding the optimum scale to close the water loop and create a balanced water flow. This can be achieved on the scale of a region, city, neighborhood, or a building. Closed-loop water systems seek to return as much water as they take from any natural flow. The ten innovations presented here reflect the understanding that in almost all circumstances all four of these scales will need to work together and that the state of water balance is something that can take years to be achieved. The goal of water managers and policy makers should be to explore the innovations presented and find tools that allow for locally achievable water systems.

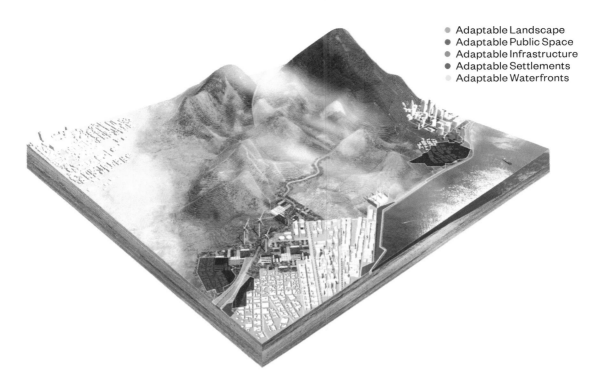

- Adaptable Landscape
- Adaptable Public Space
- Adaptable Infrastructure
- Adaptable Settlements
- Adaptable Waterfronts

There are a number of components of urban systems that can be designed to adapt to future conditions. This flexibility of use is critical in the face of predictable change and can allow planners and decision makers to dedicate clear zones and uses that are allowed to change to accommodate future demands.

Both central nodes of infrastructural investment as well as more localized interventions present an opportunity to layer in other beneficial components such as public space, ecological regeneration, and local economic opportunities.

Bundling at District Scale

By bundling infrastructure functions, it is possible to treat wastewater as a resource for creating energy, providing public space for community interaction, and providing water and energy in ways that reduce carbon emissions. By addressing cities at the district scale (defined as an area as small as two buildings or as large as a neighborhood) infrastructure systems can become more localized and resilient while providing opportunities for community engagement and learning. Focusing on the district scale allows for more site-specificity and local context. These innovations highlight the performative functions of ecology, introduce mechanical functions of co-optimized systems and adaptable infrastructure, and discuss the role of vision and leadership in making these innovations more widely implemented and accepted by groups across the socioeconomic spectrum.

Water-Energy-Waste Flows

The innovations put forth in this publication are focused on water; however, solid waste, energy, and wastewater flows are often closely related. When water is produced and distributed, there are energy costs and created emissions. The collection and treatment of these emissions also use energy. The production and distribution of energy necessitates high volumes of water. The embedded water in energy use is higher in more arid areas and lower where water is more plentiful. With the understanding of the interconnectedness of these three systems, opportunities to improve our urban water systems are the primary focus.

Urban Greening and Urban Cooling

Healthy urban ecology as a tool of resilient development and value creation needs to contribute to climate change mitigation through heat island effect reduction and stimulation of a healthy water cycle. Introduction of permeable pavement allows for stormwater absorption; this results in surface runoff retention that addresses flood and drought control, CSO control, and aquifer recharge. Stormwater collection is another resilient strategy for reducing surface runoff that can help with provision of alternative sources of water, including irrigation. Both of these strategies consider stormwater a resource rather than a nuisance that needs to be piped out as quickly as possible. These strategies slow down the water and aid in greening and forestation. Collection ponds, various water features, vegetated swales, green streets, networks of lush urban parks, waterfront promenades – the introduction of these urban interventions creates carbon sinks that lower the temperature of the air, which makes surrounding areas more habitable and more valuable. Most importantly, these small-scale measures will result in multiple benefits at a large scale.

1 Adaptable Landscape
2 Adaptable Public Space
3 Adaptable Infrastructure
4 Adaptable Settlements

Defined districts that operate around boundaries that relate to specific water infra-structure (e.g. water reuse district) can be the starting point for integrated funding and community stewardship opportunities.

Urban greening (the planting of coordinated and interconnected network of greenways and open spaces) allows for both air quality improvements and urban cooling (urban temperature moderation to reduce urban heat island effect).

FRAMEWORK DIAGRAM

Risks

Responses

RISK 1
SANITATION

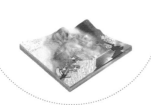

RISK 5
AGING INFRASTRUCTURE

RESPONSE 1
ADAPTABILITY

RISK 2
SLR FLOODS

RISK 6
SOLID WASTE POLLUTION

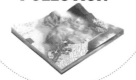

RESPONSE 2
MULTI-FUNCTIONAL & CLOSED LOOPS

RISK 3
RIVERINE FLOODS

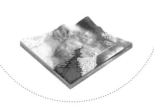

RISK 7
URBAN HARDENING & HEATING

RESPONSE 3
DISTRICTS

RISK 4
DROUGHT

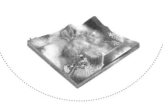

RESPONSE 4
URBAN GREENING & COOLING

Innovations

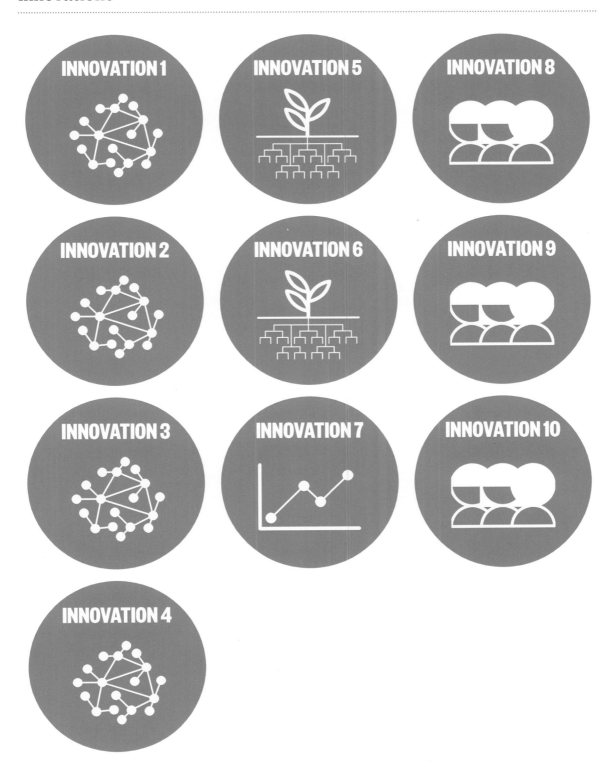

INNOVATION 1

INNOVATION 5

INNOVATION 8

INNOVATION 2

INNOVATION 6

INNOVATION 9

INNOVATION 3

INNOVATION 7

INNOVATION 10

INNOVATION 4

PART 3

Key Policy Principles

The work of our engagement process in the development of this publication focuses on developing **key policy principles** that offer a versatile framework for leaders to bring forward in their communities.

The two leading principles from our work are as follows:

1 Promote multifunctional and adaptable water infrastructure that simultaneously supports ecology and provides public space, bringing multiple benefits to urban dwellers and ensuring armatures for more resilient cities. These investments should pay special attention to water access as a women's issue, as well as increase community ownership and pride.

2 Support new value creation models by advancing integrated ecological water systems for regenerative benefits.

In more detail, urban water investments should support...

Multifunctional and Adaptable Systems that:

- Integrate local culture and traditions.
- Are inclusive of vulnerable populations.
- Transform locally undesirable land use into a desirable community asset.
- Create high performance ecology.
- Supply multiple benefits to communities.
- Are adaptable to population growth, urbanization, and climate change.
- Support intact ecological systems, including the preservation of greenfield sites.
- Provide quality public spaces for community interaction.
- Provide response systems for more resilient cities.
- Allow for the bundling of infrastructure functions.
- Treat waste as a resource for creating energy.
- Reduce carbon emissions.

Decentralized District Systems that:

- Are more localized and resilient.
- Allow for local control of critical resources.
- Provide opportunities for community engagement and learning.
- Provide a networked system of infrastructural assets that can be deployed both independently and collectively.

Value Creation Opportunities that:

- Prioritize multiple lines of defense to promote resilience.
- Use a combination of "hard" and "soft" infrastructure.
- Support interdependent centralized and decentralized systems.
- Recognize that localization and site-specificity is necessary; no single universal solution should be promoted.
- Should be used across all projects.
- Provide economic assets and opportunities.

PART 4

Ten Innovation Urban Water Infrastruc

s in

ture

The innovation strategies have been organized to facilitate the implementation by policy makers, designers, and decision makers in a variety of contexts. The innovations put forth in this publication recognize the differences in conditions of informal and formal development in developing and developed regions and can be adjusted to meet the unique conditions of every site. This document organizes the innovations into four categories:

TECHNOLOGY

ECOLOGY

FINANCE

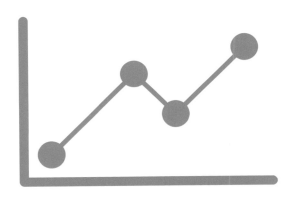

EQUITY

TECHNOLOGY

Key Policy Recommendations

Decentralized District Systems

- Prioritize water infrastructure investments to support district water systems that offer the ability to close water loops driving onsite balanced water flows, known as net zero water, while reducing disaster exposure and reducing energy intensity found in standard pump/treat/pump systems.

- Work with communities to reduce the need to purchase outside services and resources by prioritizing water infrastructure investments that capture waste nutrients from water flows as a resource to be reused as fertilizers, fuels, electricity, etc.

Adaptability of Systems

- Prioritize the deployment of infrastructure solutions that can rapidly adapt to dynamics both anticipated and unanticipated. Systems selected must protect the users from cost escalation above 3 percent per year. Within this cost structure, systems should simultaneously have the ability to upgrade for protection against future risks currently quantifiable (such as flood or climate impacts).

- Additional facilities should be planned with flexibility to adapt to some degree of future unknowns with proper space and connection options to allow facilities planners to replace the fail/demolish/replace model with a learn/optimize/evolve model. Water infrastructure systems should be configured for adaptable technologies to close water/nutrient/carbon cycles, address evolving climate risks, and reduce detrimental environmental impacts.

Data as a Tool

- Deploy data communications and response systems to protect water supplies and wastewater infrastructure from sea level rise and natural disasters.

- Support the opportunity for individual and community response to environmental dynamics through data sharing and transparency.

- Use data to develop a rapid, dynamic response to problems or fluctuations within the system.

Critical Risks for this Category

Central System Failure

- Long-term failure and expense of centralized systems

- Centralized infrastructure's lack of flexibility to adapt to changing social and environmental conditions

- Grid failure or utility service loss due to unreliability, disaster, or other critical event

- Centralized systems improvements exceed available budgets

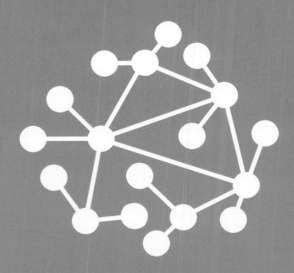

INTEGRATED MICRO-INFRASTRUCTURE CENTERS (IMICS)
RESOURCE CO-OPTIMIZATION AT SCALE & DENSITY
ADAPTABLE INFRASTRUCTURE PLATFORMS (AIPS) & BOLT-ON TECHNOLOGY (BOTS)
UTILIZATION OF DISPERSED & MOBILE TECHNOLOGY FOR SMART INFRASTRUCTURE

Critical Risks for this Category (cont'd)

Disadvantaged Populations Face Disproportionate Risks

- Poorest communities suffer inequitable exposure to infrastructure pollution and outright failure

- Inequitable access to resources for populations at risk

- Low-lying non-mobile populations threatened by sea level rise and terrestrial/riverine flooding

- Unequal access to clean water, sanitation, and energy

Compounding Factors

- Water and energy infrastructure experiencing risk, often due to cross-demand

- Rapid obsolescence of infrastructure due to accelerating innovation, changing design conditions, and long planning / construction cycles

- Dramatic inefficiencies in systems operations and significant losses due to undetected conveyance inefficiencies

- Lack of "smart" controls and communication systems prevent full utilization of infrastructure capacity or protection of certain communities from risk

INNOVATION  1

Centralized infrastructure systems are aging and costly to maintain. In aggregate, distributed infrastructural systems can replace or complement centralized systems to achieve or exceed the functional objectives of these systems. Innovation in this area revolves around publicly or privately owned water systems that provide drinking water, treat wastewater, and produce energy. These systems provide for their local context while providing resilience to the larger network.

The essential development required is the creation of context-sensitive, easily deployable modular systems. These systems can also bundle water, energy, and waste flows. They operate similarly to central utility plants and offer the flexibility of being grid independent. Finding a way to integrate distributed water systems in decentralized contexts allows water systems to perform at an overall higher efficiency while offering redundancy in the case of centralized failure or risks. Distributed water systems offer the ability to close water loops driving balanced water flows, known as net zero water, while reducing disaster exposure and energy intensity found in elaborate pump/treat/pump systems. Water IMICs are utility nodes that can operate independent of the water grid but can also plug into it when needed. IMICs reduce incremental investment necessary to build and maintain infrastructure and diversify infrastructure investment portfolios and funding structures offering increased regional autonomy and community-based control.

Resultant Outcomes for Decision Makers

Redundant systems become a form of adaptation and increase functional reliability by safeguarding communities from the excessive challenges associated with climate risk including increased availability of drinking water, low carbon water treatment, and synergies with on-site energy production. Providing a stronger set of tools for community cohesion and resiliency (local control of water resources, redundancy) allows households to adopt and help complete the water infrastructure systems on which they rely. This level of access on a personal level promotes communal inter-action (neighbors sharing the success and progress of different designs). Adoption allows communities to seek infrastructure that is cost effective to manufacture and maintain. It gives communities freedom to choose systems that best represent specific cultural and personal concerns. Placement of infrastructure centers in the urban fabric must be done in a manner that reveals resiliency benefits to users. Social, gender, and environmental justice equity factors must be addressed. Infrastructure design should be aesthetically pleasing to be accepted into the community. Place-based, site-specific design applications to increase user literacy of local contextual infrastructure systems are also important.

INTEGRATED MICRO-INFRASTRUCTURE CENTERS (IMICS)

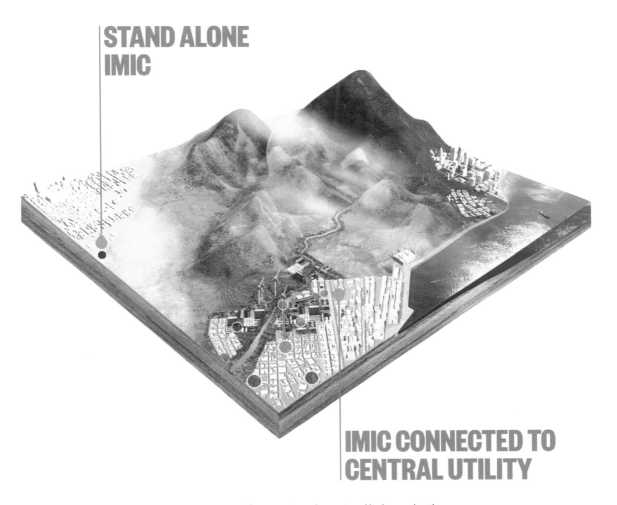

STAND ALONE
IMIC

IMIC CONNECTED TO
CENTRAL UTILITY

These facilities can support a spectrum of contexts and can stand independently as a localized utility or can be situated in proximity to a centralized system in order to augment its function.

INNOVATION  1

Applications of these Innovations Include:

Incentivize District-Scale and Building-Scale Water Plants (that Provide Drinking Water or Usable Non-Potable Water)

- Local potable water can originate from rain capture and treatment
- District wastewater recovery and blending for reuse should be stimulated
- Decentralized storm water recovery and reuse needs to be integrated into the design

Systems Process Multiple Infrastructural Functions

- Systems can also process waste and provide energy
- Can be paired with evolved conveyance systems (e.g. low pressure sewer conveyance system to reduce depth and diameter associated with traditional gravity systems)

These Facilities Should be Collocated to Provide Public Space

Advanced Levels of Technology Should be Used for Localized Control

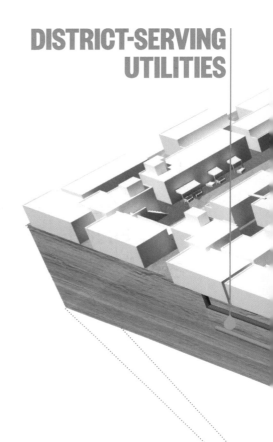

DISTRICT-SERVING UTILITIES

INTEGRATED MICRO-INFRASTRUCTURE CENTERS (IMICS)

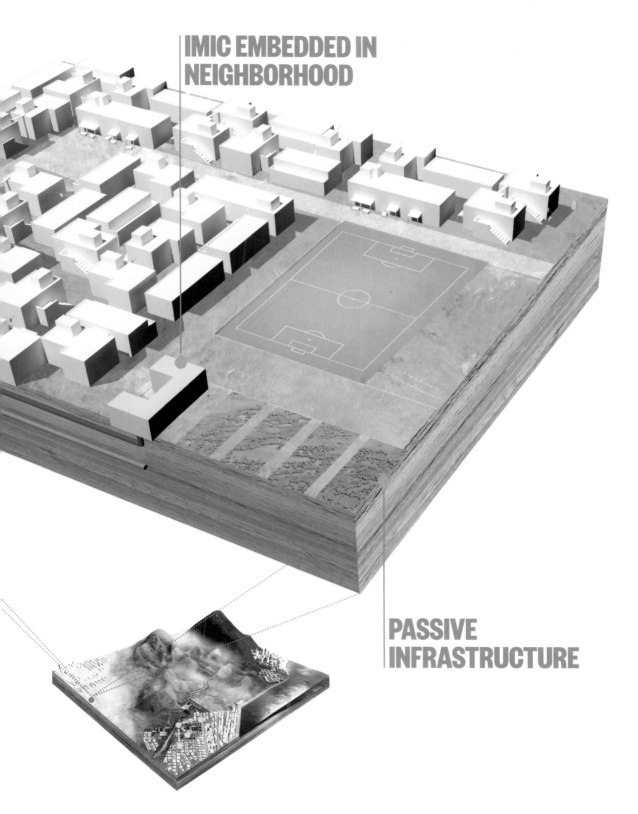

IMIC EMBEDDED IN NEIGHBORHOOD

PASSIVE INFRASTRUCTURE

 A bio-digester in a dense urban context supports the community with gas and fertilizer. This standalone system supports the community as a piece of independent infrastructure.

INTEGRATED MICRO-INFRASTRUCTURE CENTERS (IMICS)

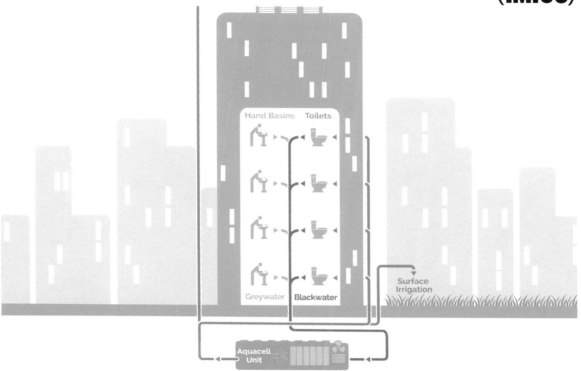

An IMIC can operate at the building scale and augment the performance of the community systems around it by reducing the load on the public infrastructure.

Dewats is a community-managed decentralized wastewater treatment system implemented in dense urban slums such as the neighborhood pictured above in Makassar, Indonesia. Dewats is a solution to eradicate open defecation and improve sanitation until full municipal wastewater treatment is feasible.

INTEGRATED MICRO-INFRASTRUCTURE CENTERS (IMICS)

 This district utility was retrofitted to recover waste heat from water used in energy production. The redesign of the site includes an architectural design, public art, and public space in the form of community gardens.

Implementation Tips

- Create a template for slums as they expand into new areas to include a model grid for new development in developing regions, including green infrastructure wastewater treatment, stormwater collection/absorption, and potable water supply. This could function like a flat-pack, which is easily distributed and assembled, and can be adjusted with materials available at a particular site.
- Micro-grid electrical and water/energy co-optimization can be the right lever to trigger these projects.
- Governance, ownership, and code barriers need to be overcome as many zoning and building restrictions prohibit the deployment of IMICs in locations conducive to optimal performance.

INNOVATION  2

Resource co-optimization occurs where more than one traditional infrastructural objective is achieved through integrated design synergies. The focus of this innovation is on the opportunity to combine one or more typical silos of infrastructure systems with a water system to expand benefits, cost sharing, and performance. This can be implemented as an integrated water utility (IWU). New multi-system IWU models offer integrated services and are funded by monetization of multi-benefits (e.g. regulatory, CSO reduction, carbon reduction).

The costs of infrastructure are rising and require innovation that can produce multiple resource flows with single investments. Energy and waste resource systems can be combined with water infrastructure to increase performance. Additionally, water infrastructure systems that are typically separated can be managed in series or optimized in conjunction with another system to augment mutual benefits (i.e. recycled water and storm water blending for non-potable reuse). IWUs link different systems together and can leverage more than one funding source to increase community buy-in.

Resultant Outcomes for Decision Makers

Co-optimized systems can help a community reduce its need to purchase outside services and resources. Capturing waste nutrients as a resource to be reused as fertilizers, fuels, and electricity, or to generate excess utility capacity, provides potential financial benefits. Other benefits include: access to nature, biophilia, capture of ecological services, energy efficient water treatment, and conveyance infrastructure. This kind of infrastructure can also attract public funds and related community support for the initiatives.

Co-optimized systems are able to provide some offline capacity when centralized systems diminish or fail because they are tied into the grid and can receive and send resources. Ecological system flows do double duty wherever landscapes perform relevant infrastructure functions while also providing increased access to nature.

RESOURCE CO-OPTIMIZATION AT SCALE & DENSITY

CO-OPTIMIZED SYSTEM AT THE CENTRAL UTILITY PLANT

RESOURCE EXCHANGE AT THE URBAN EDGE

Applications of these Innovations Include:

Linked systems added to a water plant or treatment node

- Fertilizers, nutrient, and new materials extracted from wastewater
- Fuel and renewable energy generated from process
- Direct integration of agriculture or aquaculture to benefit from resources and economize on transport distances

Linking productivity of integrated systems such as energy/water, water/ecology, water/nutrients, or water/heat

- Energy and water regional demands reduced by finding efficiencies through co-location, spatial co-location of energy and water management hubs within urban fabric
- Water-efficient cooling systems and energy production applications
- Pumping water into gravity tanks during times of surplus energy to maintain constant pressure even when energy is not available (water storage as energy battery)

Public open space integration

- Landscape, storm water, integrated open space
- Water utility in a public space

District water share across property lines

Recycled water and storm water blending for reuse

Routine use of non-potable water for non-human consumption purposes such as flushing and irrigation

Carbon management as part of ecological water system

 The Central Corridor EcoDistrict in San Francisco is characterized as a high-performance area where many systems are optimized. The earliest water project in the district was at Mint Plaza, a location where ecology treats stormwater that recharges the aquifer and at the same time is a place for public art and flexible public space.

East Kolkata Wetlands is a response to the absence of piped sewer infrastructure. Canals convey sewage from the city into an aquaculture system that treats sewage and produces food. The wetland covers 7,500 acres and processes 145 million gallons of raw sewage and stormwater every day.

SOIL is a container-based sanitation model implemented in dense urban slums in Haiti. As a method to reduce water pollution in local supplies, the program also becomes a micro-enterprise where customers pay to use the toilet, and the owner maintains the urine-separating toilets to produce compost. Monitoring and evaluation ensures the compost is safe to apply to crops and gardens.

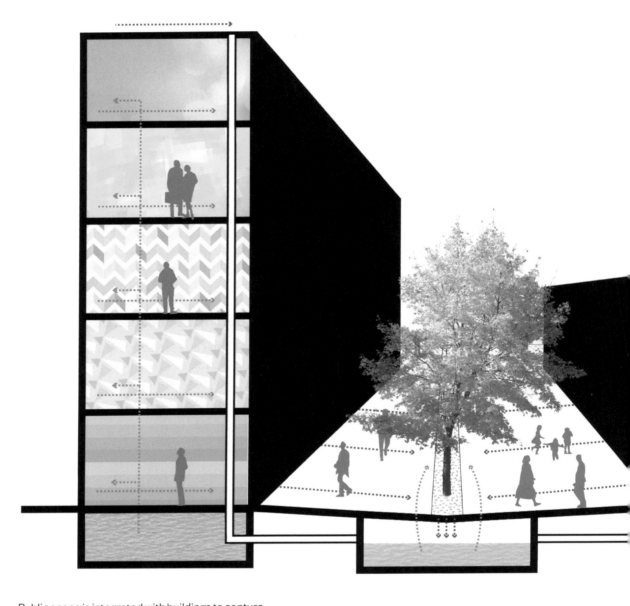

Public space is integrated with buildings to capture stormwater and graywater and blend it for non-potable reuse for irrigation.

Implementation Tips

- Encourage co-optimization of systems design for all international bank investment programs (water, energy, sanitation, etc.).

- Recognize the need to link capital investment with operating cost budgets to achieve high performance lifecycle benefits; look at distributed generation and resource benefits model; monetize social benefits of high performance such as carbon neutrality.

- Encourage private investments linkage to public infrastructure investments.

- Public Private Partnerships should be incentivized: transfer lessons learned in other countries (UK, Canada, and Australia) to other markets.

- New funding sources are needed; a possible model could be commercial PACE (Property-Assessed Clean Energy): ten to twenty year amortized property tax assessment that funds any energy efficiency, renewable energy, or water conservation systems and measures.

- Co-optimized projects need to be structured to maintain high perfor-mance benefits, not simply service benefits.

- Municipalities need to support advancements in related local testing, regulation, codes, and technologies.

- Aggregate resource impacts need to be considered within a single design/ engineering framework.

INNOVATION  3

Innovations in infrastructure require systems to be adaptable and affordable. They must have an intrinsic ability to accept iterative improvements to respond to fluctuations in climate variables; they must demand shifts, regulatory changes, resource availability, and opportunities for new technologies. Adaptable Infrastructure Platforms (or AIPs) are flexible utility nodes that operate as a chassis to allow future connections to evolve with changing needs. Their counterpart, Bolt-On Technologies (or BOTs), are future systems that allow a utility node to change its performance characteristics in response to changing supply, demand, or climate/resource variables.

The one thing we can predict about the requirements of future water management infrastructure systems is that those requirements will change. Water management systems referenced here include both urban water infrastructure and flood water management. AIPs/BOTs allow the deployment of infrastructure solutions that can rapidly advance to dynamics both anticipated and unanticipated. They address the rising relative cost of infrastructure development while simultaneously reducing the cost of water, energy, and waste. They allow for adaptability, future-proofing, and cost-effective system evolutions. They replace the fail/demolish/replace model with the learn/optimize/evolve model. They allow for learning and evolution, responding in real-time to feedback. Where there is neither time nor money to completely reconceptualize the systems that we have in place, we look towards BOTs that can adapt existing infrastructure to future needs while anticipating changing environments.

Resultant Outcomes for Decision Makers

Systems that allow for adaptation and evolution as new technologies emerge give municipalities flexibility in managing infrastructure. Successful implementation of the next generation of municipal infrastructure systems can be achieved with BOTs planned for overlapping retirement. This allows communities to continually develop productivity as population needs change.

Anticipating the needs of changing populations, while addressing water scarcity, food security, and low-carbon solutions, is key. AIPs and BOTs support existing centralized systems until those systems are replaced. Experimenting with design for possible greater capacity gains opens more opportunities for utility managers. Immediate access to new technologies and processes limits financial risk and service impacts to any part of the system. This adaptive management allows urban support systems to grow with their populations.

ADAPTABLE INFRASTRUCTURE PLATFORMS (AIPS) & BOLT-ON TECHNOLOGY (BOTS)

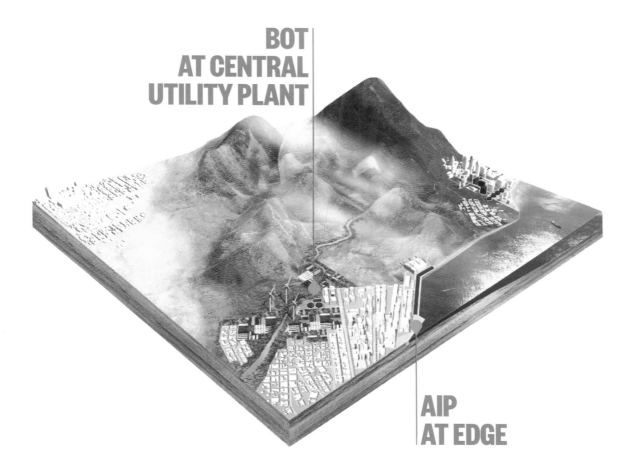

BOT
AT CENTRAL
UTILITY PLANT

AIP
AT EDGE

These facilities can support a spectrum of contexts and can stand independently as a localized utility or can be situated in proximity to a centralized system in order to augment its function.

Applications of these Innovations Include:

Utility nodes (AIPs)

- Water and wastewater infrastructure that is resilient to sea level rise and natural disasters
- Multiple input and multiple output water plants that allow for variable sources and demands over time.
- Wastewater treatment systems paired with variable resource recovery applications

Add-ons to existing central infra-structure (BOTs)

- Universal points of connection that can be utilized for multiple generations of technology development
- Alternates to seawalls including "soft" approaches that double as marine, dynamic deployable barriers
- Incremental floodwall extension
- Wastewater process for resource recovery
- Store water with gravity pressure to decouple energy dependence associated with use of pumps

ADAPTABLE INFRASTRUCTURE PLATFORMS (AIPS) & BOLT-ON TECHNOLOGY (BOTS)

INNOVATION 3

WATER FROM ELEVATED ROADWAY

 A unique prototype for adapting public infrastructure, DLANDstudio's HOLD (Highway Outfall Landscape Detention) system captures stormwater runoff from elevated highways and sends it to a modular passive treatment system to remove pollutants from the roadway.

ADAPTABLE INFRASTRUCTURE PLATFORMS (AIPS) & BOLT-ON TECHNOLOGY (BOTS)

Lotus Water produces hand pumps that disinfect water automatically at the withdrawal location without additional steps or the use of energy. Innovations that can be deployed in a distributed manner can fulfill a critical public health function.

IN: WASTEWATER

OUT: TREATED WASTEWATER

Algae bags float on the water's surface, processing wastewater for a few days before pumping into the plant for refining. This system treats wastewater with algae and produces carbon negative fuels, potable water, and fertilizers.

ADAPTABLE INFRASTRUCTURE PLATFORMS (AIPS) & BOLT-ON TECHNOLOGY (BOTS)

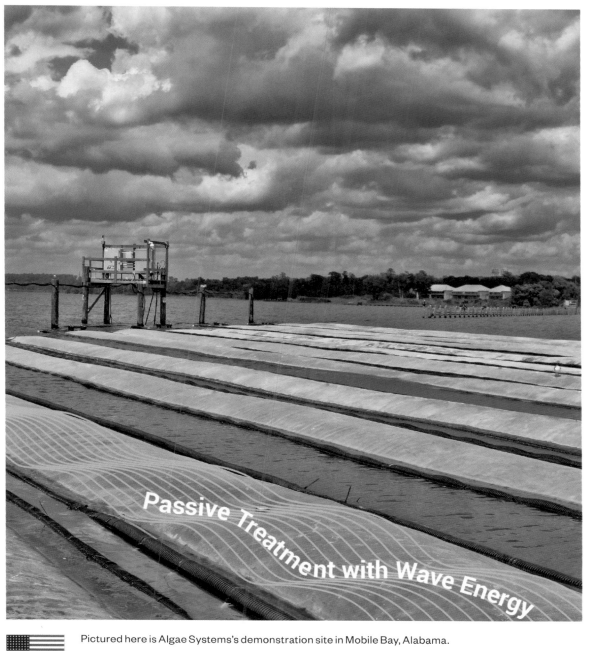

Passive Treatment with Wave Energy

 Pictured here is Algae Systems's demonstration site in Mobile Bay, Alabama.

 Electricity is generated from turbines placed in gravity-fed pipes bringing drinking water from the Mt. Hood watershed to Portland.

ADAPTABLE INFRASTRUCTURE PLATFORMS (AIPS) & BOLT-ON TECHNOLOGY (BOTS)

In Haiti, a network of hygiene points knows as "Simbi Hubs" is planned to provide localized sanitation processes. Each Simbi Hub includes areas for lavatories, bathing, and laundry, as well as facilities for food storing and preparation. Water and sewage are treated on site and the hubs address issues relating to storm drainage and earthquake safety. All elements required to build the new infrastructure are designed to be made locally, using established craft skills.

Implementation Tips

- Design water and electric utilities that function as carbon negative systems, implementing resource and water recovery that are energy positive and revenue-generating operations.
- Develop options for adaptable technologies to close water/ nutrient/ carbon cycles, address evolving climate risks, and reduce detrimental environmental impacts.
- Improve ability to project future innovation and necessary support/ integration of systems.
- Size long-term baseline systems needs to accommodate future growth.
- Balance short and long-term investments.
- Support opportunities to incorporate experimental technology reliability and economics; allow for some infrastructure components to have a long adoption cycle, from concept to pilot to scale; address the need-accelerated adoption of new technology innovation that can be validated.
- Allow for systems to evolve and for replacement of parts over time.

INNOVATION  4

There is an opportunity to advance the available data, controls, and management of infrastructure more efficiently through the introduction of technology. Sensing and monitoring can be used to reflect infrastructure functionality or highlight where there might be issues. Intrinsic to these systems is the opportunity for individual and community response to environmental dynamics through data sharing and transparency.

Poor and low-lying communities bear an inordinate share of infrastructure and water resource limitations. Key opportunities lie in improved system performance with distributed controls and communications for those communities to make informed decisions quickly. Timely communication of resource flows, risks, and information availability is key to implementing a secure utility supply and protecting communities from risk (flooding, contamination, etc.). Leveraging existing widespread smart technology amongst the public to improve data flow to infrastructure managers and automated central controls will also help effective decisions to be made in a more responsive manner. And to help urban systems to best serve growing populations, multivalent urban space is required for accepting infrastructural flexibility and indeterminacy.

Resultant Outcomes for Decision Makers

Interaction between modeling and sensing data allows community needs to be better tracked, understood, and reacted to. Using data to develop a rapid, dynamic response to problems or fluctuations within the system is key. Data is increasingly available to help system operators understand population needs and scale up or scale down supporting infrastructure; support of this emerging software allows for effective aggregation and interpretation of large data inputs.

UTILIZATION OF DISPERSED & MOBILE TECHNOLOGY FOR SMART INFRASTRUCTURE

INNOVATION  4

Applications of these Innovations Include:

Warning Systems

- Use sensors and a linked transparent reporting data system to measure pollution concentrations in water systems and resources. When levels pass a threshold, mobile tech can be used to notify the proper agency, communicate to the public, and/or send an automated response.
- Pre-alert of potential sewer overflow contamination threat would allow people to limit water use to prevent an overflow.
- Use mobile technology to send information to government agencies to let them know about localized water shortages and other real-time disruptions.
- Pre-alert of potential threat (or other user-controllable infrastructure failure) to change behavior to encourage conservation to prevent the event from happening, which would keep raw sewage out of water bodies and improve water quality.

Communications/ Monitoring to Increase Performance of Infrastructure

- Reliable monitoring and control systems for effective water resource management can be introduced.
- Predictive modeling using meta data analysis can be encouraged.
- Decentralized storm water controls can manage flooding and desynchronize peak flows with quality data of high granularity.
- Distributed communications empower discrete users (e.g. smart hand pumps that send information to mobile phones to indicate when the pump is broken).
- Hardware for implementing new smart technologies is needed.

UTILIZATION OF DISPERSED & MOBILE TECHNOLOGY FOR SMART INFRASTRUCTURE

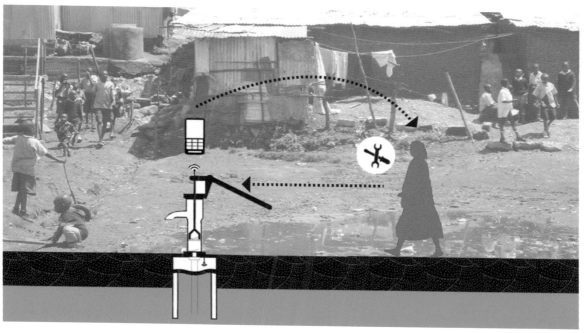

 One-third of hand pumps in developing nations may be broken at any one time. "Smart hand pumps" automatically transmit water use and performance data over mobile networks, sending text message alerts of breakdowns.

 Women in informal settlements in Luanda, Angola use cell phones to see where drinking water is available. This program has brought down the price of water.

 Sensor networks can be used for monitoring and responding to environmental dynamics. Data accessed via cell phone can inform a fisherman about the demand at various markets so he can see where he can make the most money from his fish. Networks can also be used to find access to better water quality.

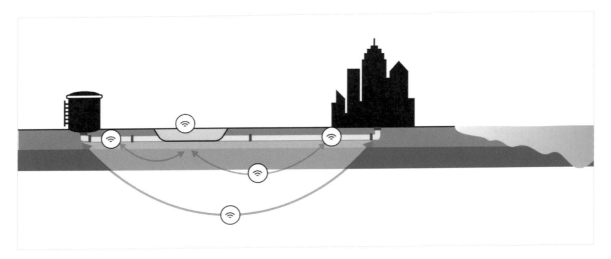

A sensing network embedded throughout a municipal water delivery system can identify aspects useful to water management such as demand, flow rate, and repair needs.

UTILIZATION OF DISPERSED & MOBILE TECHNOLOGY FOR SMART INFRASTRUCTURE

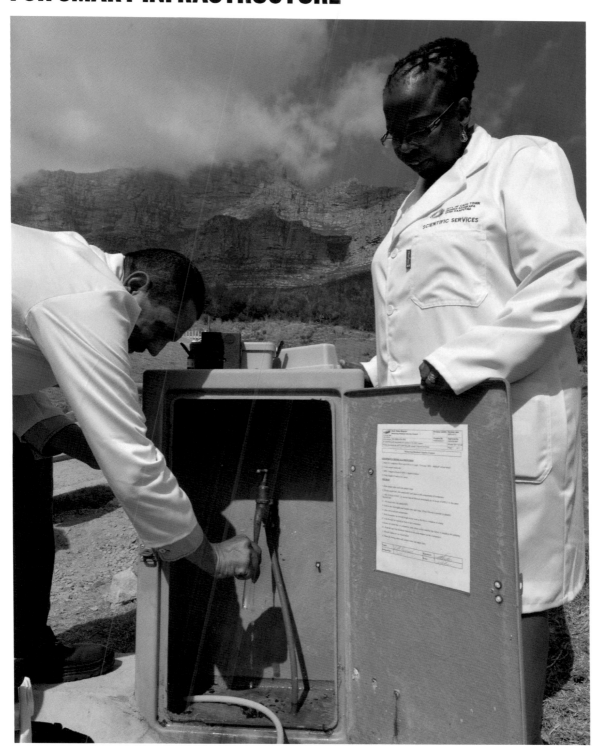

Water Quality Reporter is an app that allows people to report water quality information via SMS and is used to ensure household drinking water is safe for consumption. Authorities within the Water Care Units of municipalities in Capetown, South Africa use this information to follow up on sites that are not complying with proper water treatment.

 Singapore's sensor network provides monitoring and control of water resources to reduce the amount of non-revenue water. A digital dashboard uses mapping and real time data to support the Public Utilities Board in making decisions related to water management.

Sensing devices are used to provide data to support managing Singapore's water infrastructure.

UTILIZATION OF DISPERSED & MOBILE TECHNOLOGY FOR SMART INFRASTRUCTURE

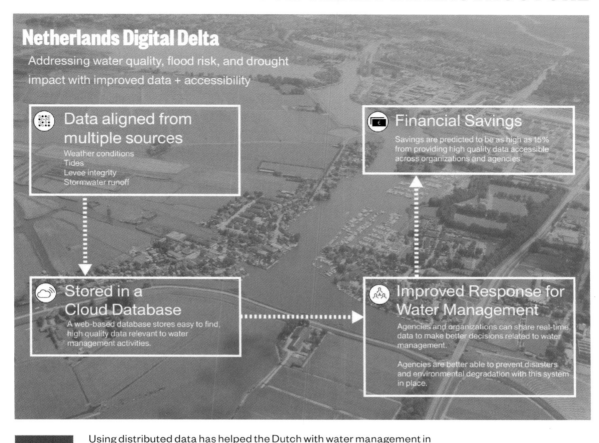

Netherlands Digital Delta

Addressing water quality, flood risk, and drought impact with improved data + accessibility

Data aligned from multiple sources
Weather conditions
Tides
Levee integrity
Stormwater runoff

Financial Savings
Savings are predicted to be as high as 15% from providing high quality data accessible across organizations and agencies.

Stored in a Cloud Database
A web-based database stores easy to find, high quality data relevant to water management activities.

Improved Response for Water Management
Agencies and organizations can share real-time data to make better decisions related to water management.

Agencies are better able to prevent disasters and environmental degradation with this system in place.

Using distributed data has helped the Dutch with water management in their high flood risk areas.

Implementation Tips

- Plan for solutions that require city integrated infrastructure if response technology is to be effective.
- Recognize the need for higher resolution data and information sets to improve efficiency.
- Be advised that increased awareness may negatively impact informal users by exposing unofficial access to resources; in some cases large populations could lose access to resources, raising other significant civic issues.
- Look for technological infrastructure funding to better address flooding, drought, and urban heat island impact from climate change.

ECOLOGY

Key Policy Recommendations

Spatial Planning of Cities

- Implement policies that rethink and update the structural urban geometry to capture passive ecological benefits, increase resiliency, and reduce the load on mechanical technology to provide comfort and sustainable resource utilization. This could include development setback from risk areas, development right transfer mechanisms, and other policy tools.

- Support the development of new urban structures that incorporate dynamic landscape systems as part of their spatial plans. Develop a city "greenprint," that is a document that incorporates high performance ecology interlinked with development adjusted for scale and context.

- Develop a kit of parts as part of the greenprint allowing for varying-sized ecological modules to plug into urban spatial structures as they are redeveloped or built in a pristine setting.

Critical Risks for this Category

As ecological systems are compromised or collapse, the subsequent loss of biodiversity has direct impacts on the economic viability of urban growth. Yet economic models ignore the true cost of impacts by not accounting for the role of ecology in our cities. This can be addressed by embedding access to nature in the evolutionary footprints of cities as they expand and densify. Planning for and designing space to incorporate ecological systems provides value such as ecological benefits and increased property values. New value creation models can transfer regional benefits accrued to individual actors responsible for transformation of a district, system, or urban mechanism. Valuation of regional resilience to scalar contributors holds a key in this additive process. The critical risks we are addressing in this chapter are:

Ecological

Ecological systems collapse, loss of biodiversity. The loss of healthy environment impacts for human health and urban performance.

Economic

Current economic models ignore the true cost of impacts. Gray infrastructure-dominated cities have a high exposure to above risks.

Human Experience and Health Risk

Expanding cities lack access to nature and public open space. Low-lying non-mobile populations are threatened by sea level rise and terrestrial/ riverine flooding. Urban air and water quality are declining. Cities are overheating.

INTEGRATION OF HIGH PERFORMANCE ECOLOGY IN AN URBAN CONTEXT

NEW VALUE-CREATION MODELS: ADDRESSING URBAN / ECOLOGICAL RISK

INNOVATION 🌱 5

Creating ecological/ functional open spaces improves our human habitats while enhancing urban buffers against climate risks. Incorporation of these elements can sustain healthier communities and improve the quality of life in connection with urbanization. Additionally, developments near bodies of water are challenged with issues of flooding, erosion, and other risks that can be ameliorated with ecological buffers.

Most existing cities and urban development occurred at the expense of ecological health, yet urban and green spaces can coexist and reinforce each other. Therefore, it is essential to rethink and update urban design and planning to capture passive ecological benefits, increase resiliency, and reduce the load on mechanical technology to provide comfort and sustainable resource utilization. Trade, industry, and habitation shaped early cities, many of which align with oceans, rivers, and lakes. Many of those systems exist today in compromised condition and increasing obsolescence. In the era of extreme climate change impacts, many existing hard-grey, engineered systems have finite utility to defend against stronger storms and other extreme weather events, sea level rise, and increased urban population densities. Development of new urban structures that engage dynamic landscape systems is an important part of the solution.

Resultant Outcomes for Decision Makers

Implementation of these strategies reduces urban risks from flooding, sea level rise, and urban heat island effect. These innovations present an opportunity to include low/no energy infrastructure into the grid. Possibly of greatest importance is the ability to create dynamic self-sustaining public spaces that enrich the environmental and social context wherever they are added.

INTEGRATION OF HIGH PERFORMANCE ECOLOGY IN AN URBAN CONTEXT

HABITAT CORRIDORS

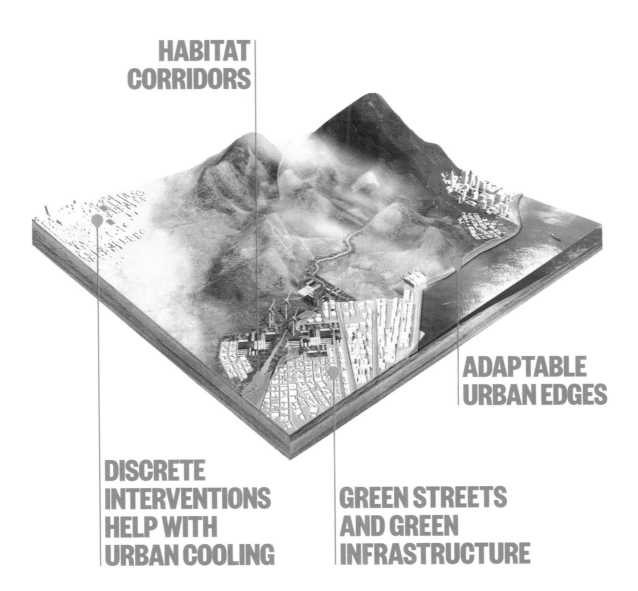

ADAPTABLE URBAN EDGES

DISCRETE INTERVENTIONS HELP WITH URBAN COOLING

GREEN STREETS AND GREEN INFRASTRUCTURE

INNOVATION 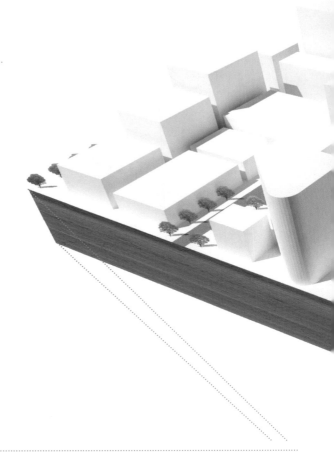 5

Applications of these Innovations Include:

Urban Risk Buffers

- Establish coastal buffer to mitigate, adapt, and protect against sea level rise and storm events; emphasize the use of horizontal levees.
- Reduce heat intensity and water needed for urban cooling.
- Increase development of floodable recreational park spaces that can manage both average and extreme city drainage flooding.
- Introduce sunken plazas within dense urban contexts to address flooding during the extreme weather events.
- Propose development of wetland edges and planted barrier islands to modulate storm surges.
- Use living breakwaters to mitigate storm surge and adapt to sea level rise.

Ecological Treatment systems

- Passive wetland treatment systems need to be integrated into accessible landscape.
- New forms of pop-up or permanent green infrastructure systems that create public open space have to be designed with higher albedo surfaces and shade structures with integrated solar capture to increase the range of functionality.
- Use misting devices and vegetation to absorb particulate matter and improve community health near roadways and industrial sites with high levels of air pollution.
- Use modular in-ground bio-swales, sponge parks, and permeable paving systems to manage storm water runoff from upland sources.
- Incentivize the use of vegetation on structure for in situ storm water control, urban heat island mitigation, and carbon reduction.

INTEGRATION OF HIGH PERFORMANCE ECOLOGY IN AN URBAN CONTEXT

PUBLIC SPACE ON URBAN EDGE PROVIDES ECOLOGICAL BUFFER TO COASTAL CLIMATE IMPACTS

INNOVATION 5

Applications of these Innovations Include (cont'd):

Human habitat enhancement

- Encourage direct wild-urban inter-action and create spaces for wildlife; reduce negative effects of density by increasing access to nature and cultivating biophilia.

- Develop a replicable "greenprint" for incorporation of high-performance ecology interlinked with development adjusted for scale and context – this requires a kit of parts that allows for varying-sized ecologically modules to plug into urban spatial structures as they are redeveloped or built on greenfield sites.

- Propose creation of varied street geometry (including integrated ecological storm water filters) to handle average storm water loads; also propose the use of streets to collect and hold larger amounts of water like a reservoir until tides and flood waters recede.

- Wherever possible introduce networks of green streets and connect the layers of urban parks.

- Improve urban acoustics by using green wall, green roof, and blue roof systems.

- Cap sunken highways to reduce air pollution, add green space for carbon sequestration, recycle water, and reduce heat island effect while increasing connectivity.

INTEGRATION OF HIGH PERFORMANCE ECOLOGY IN AN URBAN CONTEXT

The integration of wetlands within a common space on a university campus, such as University of California, Berkley above, provides stormwater functionality and a place of calm in an otherwise dense urban setting.

INNOVATION 5

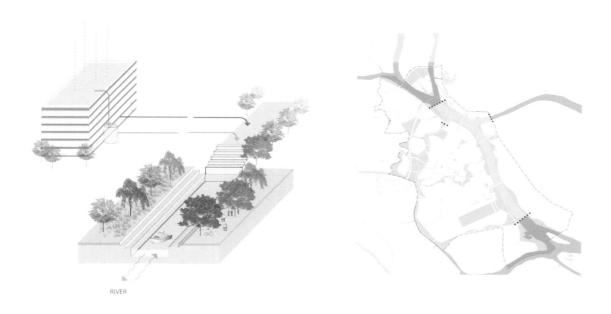

RIVER

 In Guangzhou, stormwater is captured and reused through a series of canals, green streets, and an internal park network creating "Sponge City" that absorbs water and sustains ecology.

INTEGRATION OF HIGH PERFORMANCE ECOLOGY IN AN URBAN CONTEXT

 The Horizontal Levee ® (the Bay Institute) is an alternative to the traditional levee. It has a gentler slope that allows marshland to migrate as sea levels rise while still providing protection for communities vulnerable to flooding and sea level rise.

 A linear park system creates a green corridor along the riverfront helping to provide water quality improvements to the runoff from the site and abutting neighborhood. Improvements in water quality help to improve the condition of the existing waterway and enhance the local ecosystem in the area.

INNOVATION 5

Stormwater Basins

Rain Gardens

Stormwater Tree Trenches

Infiltration Trenches

Stormwater Bumpouts

Cobbs Creek Park, a linear park system in Philadelphia, creates a green corridor along the riverfront helping to provide water quality improvements to the runoff from the site and abutting neighborhood. Improvements in water quality help to improve the condition of the existing waterway and enhance the local ecosystem in the area.

INTEGRATION OF HIGH PERFORMANCE ECOLOGY IN AN URBAN CONTEXT

Implementation Tips

- It is essential to create a dedicated funding source and management system for long-term care and stewardship of green infrastructure systems, as they are living systems that need regular maintenance.

- Develop research and metrics to analyze performance criteria associated with district and civic scale green infrastructure for the following categories: urban heat island, cooling loads, air quality, water quality, storm water runoff volumes, habitat value, carbon sequestration, coastal resiliency, and human health factors.

- Integrating living infrastructure within the built environment requires reallocation of public space.

- Provide open data and maps available for cities developing green infrastructure plans as it gets implemented.

- Develop protocols to identify and evaluate alternative approaches to retrofit infrastructure, such as integrating living infrastructure.

- Determine the location, geometry, and organization of energy, water, and information technology infrastructure for protection from flooding, enhanced urban permeability, and energy capture.

INNOVATION 🌱 6

Advancing the integration of ecological systems in an urban context, and to receive the benefit of their regenerative potential, requires the commodification and revaluation of those and adjacent assets. Such valuation and subsequent value creation models allow for economic transformation of ecological system stewardship.

Among the problems our society must solve are issues of sea level rise and climate change, air pollution, flooding, degraded water quality, and reduced water supplies. Solutions are now available that create value at the nexus of ecology and technology. Innovation and strategic investments are needed to transition our society away from a centralized "hidden" approach to managing resources and risks towards a distributed network of visible green infrastructure systems capable of reducing urban risk while enhancing communities.

Risk of ecological failure is linked to urban failure, as a function of lost ecological benefits. If our ecological systems fail, human settlements are undermined as well. Ecological benefits include but are not limited to: sea level rise response, air quality control, water supply and quality control, provision of sanitation, carbon sequestration, pathogen control, temperature modulation, and flood control. We need to protect urban settlements from these risks and enhance them with the benefits accrued from a repositioned attitude.

Optimized infrastructure can be achieved through the commodification of investments in which the cost is shared, incentives are distributed, and benefits accrue in proportion to the role or importance of the project. For example, investments in green infrastructure made by land developers accrue benefits to water and wastewater management providers by strategically investing money to replace aging infrastructure; a triple bottom line analysis can yield the benefits, the costs of which can be born by the party responsible through tax incentives, grant programs, or density bonuses. This example extends to other contexts and systems through these linked cost and benefit sharing strategies.

Desired Outcome

In aggregate, patches of living infrastructure systems provide comparable services of a large natural system. These can include urban forests, urban agriculture, and ecological water treatment systems. To these ends, floods in streams and rivers can be accommodated rather than restricted because of the benefits provided such as improved hydrology, recreational space, and habitat of other species. Populations affected by sea level rise and flooding can become stewards of functional landscapes that protect their communities. Shared investment results in shared returns to the communities investing.

NEW VALUE-CREATION MODELS: ADDRESSING URBAN / ECOLOGICAL RISK

 Brooklyn Bridge Park is designed to be floodable during storms by implementing soft edges and protection berms embedded in the formed edges as an alternative to a floodwall. The variety of spaces makes for interesting experiences in the park during the absence of heavy storms.

Applications of these Innovations Include :

Valuation of Ecological Assets

- A cap and trade system of water availability would create an allowance for customers; if the allowance is exceeded, it must be repaid.
- Develop valuation tools for understanding aggregate benefits of living infrastructure at district, civic, and regional scales.
- Introduce ecological system mitigation banking (i.e. wetland banking, rainforest banking).
- Develop monitoring techniques for new infrastructure performance.

Strategic Investments

- Replace gray infrastructure with green infrastructure.
- Support the flood protection through tidal wetland restoration to mitigate sea level rise and climate change.

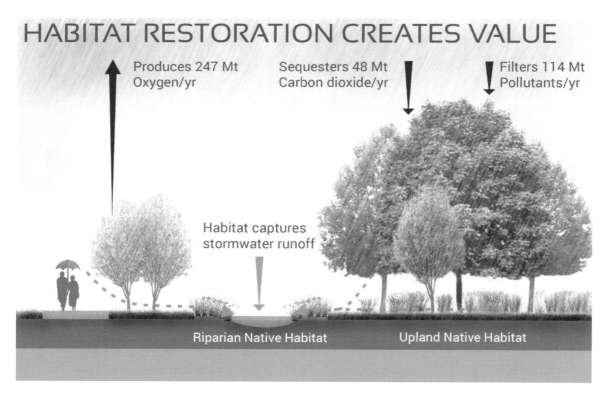

HABITAT RESTORATION CREATES VALUE

Produces 247 Mt
Oxygen/yr

Sequesters 48 Mt
Carbon dioxide/yr

Filters 114 Mt
Pollutants/yr

Habitat captures
stormwater runoff

Riparian Native Habitat

Upland Native Habitat

Integrating ecology into a site provides an improved aesthetic as well as providing ecosystem services, such as carbon sequestration and improved air quality and water quality.

NEW VALUE-CREATION MODELS: ADDRESSING URBAN / ECOLOGICAL RISK

 Cheonggyecheon, a historical waterway in Seoul, Korea was put underground with a highway built on top of it. Years later, the waterway is now daylit and has been transformed into a vibrant public space.

INNOVATION  6

 China recently released a plan to value natural resources, improve payment-based resource consumption, and compensate conservation and ecological protection efforts. This is a major move towards protecting and promoting the use of ecology for human developments.

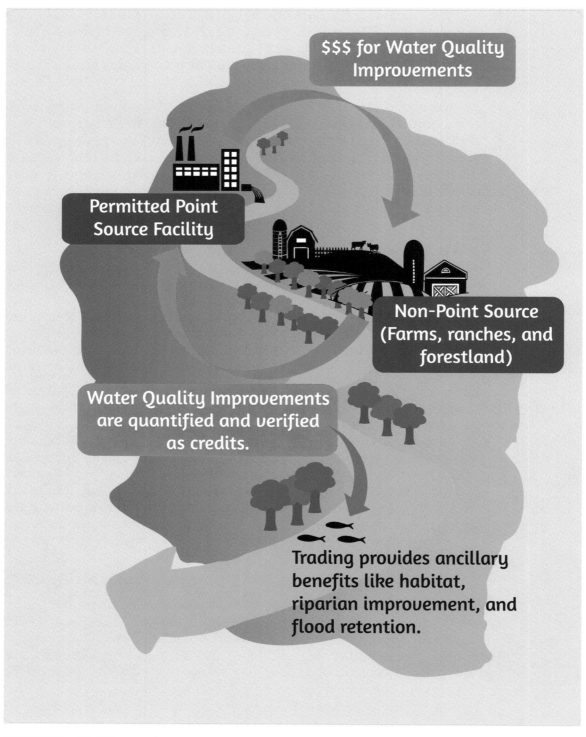

$$$ for Water Quality Improvements

Permitted Point Source Facility

Non-Point Source (Farms, ranches, and forestland)

Water Quality Improvements are quantified and verified as credits.

Trading provides ancillary benefits like habitat, riparian improvement, and flood retention.

The Willamette Partnership in Portland, Oregon is an ecosystem services accounting program that quantifies ecosystem services and creates market-based incentive programs to improve conservation outcomes. Their Ecosystem Crediting Platform is designed to be used by land managers and project developers.

NEW VALUE-CREATION MODELS: ADDRESSING URBAN / ECOLOGICAL RISK

Implementation Tips

- A combination of centralized planning frameworks coupled with distributed development controls and guidelines is required to address this relationship, again coupled with a strategic mechanism for the advancement of supportive financial structures and value-sharing arrangements. The physical expression of these innovations is achieved through financial support of quality urban planning and design. Additionally, the transformative role of post-disaster response needs to be predetermined in order to anticipate robust deployment of resources in a manner that provides maximum adherence to long-term resiliency goals. Maturation of ecological applications require planning and advanced preparation; they are not a quick fix.

- Set up systems for emergency response that shift away from the standard "hard" engineering fixes – like the flood walls implemented in New Orleans after Hurricane Katrina – towards immediate deployment of distributed strategies that combine ecological and technological components.

- Deploy monitoring technology to track the operation of these systems, potentially spread across an entire city versus the current systems that monitor central facilities. This is an opportunity to revolutionize the ways in which the public considers infrastructure. Tools can be developed to shift human expectation to accept daily interactions with the water cycle.

FINANCE

Key Policy Recommendations

New Finance Models

- Implement policy and regulatory programs that allow privately owned district-scale water system upgrades within the larger-scale public infrastructure

- Establish an ecological cap and trade system or comparable value creation model to advance the protection and integration of ecological systems in an urban context. Maximize the benefit of ecological regenerative potential by requiring the commodification and revaluation of those assets and adjacent assets.

Investment Programs

- Require co-optimized systems design for all international bank investment programs where water systems would also have to positively impact local or regional energy, sanitation, waste, or other systems.

Spatial Finance Mechanism

- Provide a discounted rate structure based on proximity to water system investments serving over one thousand people. This should be done wherever infrastructure must be planned as an amenity and wherever incentives provide an opportunity for people to build small, decentralized systems.

Critical Risks for this Category

- Long-term failure and expense of centralized systems

- Lost opportunities to benefit from new economic models and new technology that could improve infrastructure performance

- Poorest communities often suffer disproportionately from infrastructure pollution from centralized plants

- Grid failure or utility service loss due to unreliability, disaster, or other critical event

- Utility failure due to exceeded capacity for conveyance, treatment, etc.

- Underfunded public sector and consolidation of private sector wealth

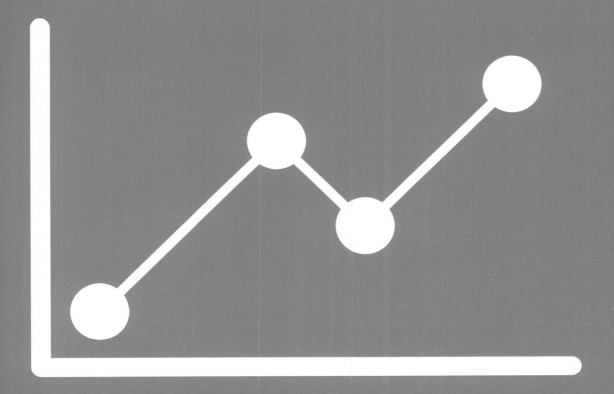

ADVANCES IN DECENTRALIZED INFRASTRUCTURE ECONOMICS

INNOVATION 7

New economic models are needed for water systems that operate at various scales complementary to or independent of centralized systems. These models present an opportunity to merge different funding streams and mechanisms where historically independent balance sheets are aligned for enhanced economic performance. Since urban water systems are moving into ever-integrated management constructs, these new economic models are necessary to support their deployment. Decentralized funding mechanisms reflect the structure of decentralized systems, putting the ownership of the system closer to the hands of the people it serves.

New models are needed to advance and allow district infrastructure to be built in order to create smaller infrastructure nodes that are more financially nimble. These need to be balanced with incremental evolution where central systems are robust, yet operating at capacity. These systems can benefit from ancillary infrastructure. Rather than upgrade the entire system, the infrastructure node can reduce the load to within the capacity of the existing primary system.

Resultant Outcomes for Decision Makers

Benefits accrue both personally and as a community. Infrastructure "ownership" can be transferred to new residents without legacy "first-here, most benefits" or "socially privileged, most benefits" ethos. Through modular financing, governance, and maintenance models local control can expand to support integration of centralized systems and associated district nodes (information, controls, hardware, ownership, financing). Financing models for public-private partnerships, including capital and operation expenses, can be merged with policy and regulatory programs for integrating privately conceived district scale upgrades with large-scale public infrastructure. Distributed mechanisms to address risks are key, including distributed financing that decreases risk in single failures.

ADVANCES IN DECENTRALIZED INFRASTRUCTURE ECONOMICS

INNOVATION  7

Applications of these Innovations Include:

Decentralized funding

- District infrastructure as economic unit that is locally financed and benefits accrued
- Public health benefits used as a driver for financing
- Public Private Partnerships for local water infrastructure (P3s)
- Decentralized power and sewer treatment plants
- Public support funding of district water infrastructure (like SFPUC in San Francisco)
- Crowd-funding to support installation and investment (like Solar Mosaic in the United States)
- Cheap and effective community based implementation (in much the same manner as Grameen Bank)

ADVANCES IN DECENTRALIZED INFRASTRUCTURE ECONOMICS

EARNING MENU

 CARE FOR COMMUNITY COMMONS

 COMMUNITY KITCHEN GARDEN

 ORGANIZING COMMUNITY EVENTS

MENTORING YOUTH

SoCC Market

REDEEMING MENU

 ELECTRICITY AND WATER BILL

 SENIOR CARE

 CHILD CARE

 USE OF COMMUNITY COMMONS

 SoCCs is a program that catalyzes development without relying on money. Is it currently being used to restore the Vaigai River, pictured here. It is a credit system based on giving value to typically unpaid labor. People earn credit for tasks carried out that benefit their neighborhood. These credits are then used for products and services in the community.

TYPICAL WASTEWATER TREATMENT

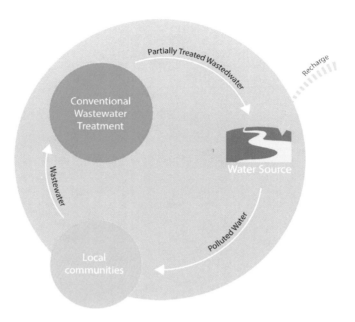

INNOVATIVE WASTEWATER TREATMENT

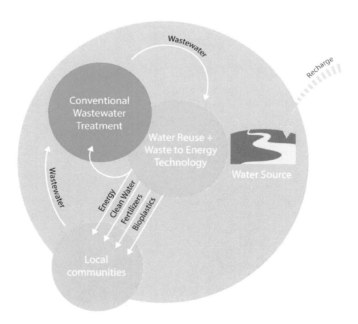

To effectively transfer to new types of technology, the water and energy industries have produced a type of partnership that reduces risk. A water energy purchase agreement (WEPA) allows a client to reduce their risk in using new technologies by implementing them on site and charging the site owner for the resources produced. The client is not burdened with the cost of maintenance of the technology, and they have locally-produced resources available for purchase, sometimes below market value.

ADVANCES IN DECENTRALIZED INFRASTRUCTURE ECONOMICS

 Citizens gather in a circle during a participatory budgeting session.

Implementation Tips

- Demand for private sector applications should be assisted through code and policy changes to allow shared infrastructure, ROW, and physicality of implementation.
- Create a system where the sites closer to a WWTP provide cheaper service than those further out. This would make the infrastructure an amenity and create an opportunity for people to build small, decentralized systems to decrease rates.

EQUITY, LEADERSHIP & GOVERNANCE

Key Policy Recommendations

Collaboration at Scale

- Create a framework for a multi-jurisdictional authority to develop solutions to address climate impacts such as sea level rise, sharing of scarce water resources, and watershed stewardship. The focus of such an authority should be to produce flexibility and equity for citizens.

Pilot First

- Support demonstration projects for small-scale public-private partnerships that engage communities in short-term achievable steps for long-term participatory success while improving livability of neighborhoods.

Social Justice

- Address social justice issues with infrastructure investments by allowing disadvantaged communities to deflect the negative impacts of wastewater and flooding infrastructure and receive maximum benefit from the resiliency benefits.

Community Ownership

- Set up legal and financial systems for community ownership of distributed water infrastructure. Personality of community can be expressed by choice of infrastructure solution and its implementation.

- Support new models for water infrastructure aligned with clear and communicable community benefits in order to gain traction and receive the stewardship necessary for their successful operation and performance. Community based infrastructure can become social and cultural assets.

Critical Risks for this Category

- Unequal access to clean water, sanitation, and energy
- Rapidly growing cities lack community access to public open space

- Poorest communities suffer disproportionate health hazards

LEADERSHIP AND VISION: LEVERAGING "COOL FACTOR" TO CREATE DISTRICT INFRASTRUCTURE

SOCIAL JUSTICE / ENVIRONMENTAL JUSTICE: COMMUNITY EMPOWERMENT & RESOURCE EQUITY

MULTI-SCALAR & JURISDICTIONAL FRAMEWORKS FOR COLLABORATION & BIOREGIONAL RESILIENCY

INNOVATION  8

Communication of a vision can be a transformative mechanism for accelerating change. New models for infrastructure must be aligned with clear and communicable community benefits in order to gain traction and receive stewardship necessary for their successful operation and performance. Community based infrastructure can become a social and cultural asset. The role of leadership is key in establishing a long-term vision and getting the short-term steps in place to begin achieving it.

There is a clear opportunity in many communities to get people with a strong vision on board. Leaders need powerful ideas to galvanize their constituents around. Putting forth a positive vision and marrying that vision with risk protection can achieve meaningful results.

Resultant Outcomes for Decision Makers

The spatial arrangement of cities needs to be inclusive and must exhibit multiple functions within urban fabric – infrastructural, agricultural, residential – so that it is safe, attractive, and compatible with regulatory stakeholders. Public space needs to be integrated as highly functional and accessible. Social cohesion, which strengthens urban resilience, is a common goal of sustainable resource development. Increased use of shared public systems ties communities to a common goal of sustainable resource development. Decision makers should build upon viable models for incorporating community design input into project funding and implementation, and develop infrastructure as a cultural asset or attraction. They should also bundle necessary infrastructure with "desirable" facilities, i.e. bundle water infrastructure with other land uses such as stormwater capture on a soccer field.

LEADERSHIP AND VISION: LEVERAGING "COOL FACTOR" TO CREATE DISTRICT INFRASTRUCTURE

The BIG U (Dryline) is a design along the waterfront edge of lower Manhattan that aims to protect the city from sea level rise. It also provides public space for active and passive recreation as well as ecological integration with the urban fabric. It is comprised of a series of interventions that will jointly engage and educate neighboring communities giving them a stake in becoming stewards of these highly performative public spaces.

INNOVATION  8

Applications of these Innovations Include :

Galvanize community around a vision

- Identify key projects that become a magnet for public adoption and engagement.
- Leverage the investments of corporate and academic campuses to enhance a larger vision for the city. Sometimes it takes a brand to carry it out before the city carries it out. Corporate and academic campuses operate at a district scale; transparency of infrastructure as a pedagogical tool speaks to the campus environment.

Engage the public through interactive urban design integration

- Think of infrastructure as a user experienced amenity. We need to envision an updated urban design aesthetic that includes district infrastructure.
- Use interactive exhibits by artists in public spaces to spark public thinking about ecological and developmental issues.
- Create temporary interventions to engage the public (use short-term intervention models as a catalyst).

Bundle community benefits with infrastructure projects

- Think about the spatial arrangement of infrastructure as part of an inclusive city design (social, residential, agricultural, etc.).
- Look for opportunities to integrate highly functional accessible public spaces.

LEADERSHIP AND VISION: LEVERAGING "COOL FACTOR" TO CREATE DISTRICT INFRASTRUCTURE

 Ned Kahn's sculpture collects rainwater and expresses water movement. Using public art to draw attention to the pressing issue of water supply can also provide a sense of beauty and attraction.

Google's data center in Douglas County, Georgia uses recycled wastewater for its cooling operations. Displaying infrastructure and design in an interesting way develops awareness of infrastructure and can be a source of pride rather than an eyesore.

LEADERSHIP AND VISION: LEVERAGING "COOL FACTOR" TO CREATE DISTRICT INFRASTRUCTURE

Implementation Tips

- Long-term vision needs to be phased and coordinated with shorter term mandates of decision makers.
- Viable models or demonstration projects are needed for small-scale public-private partnerships that engage communities for long-term participatory success while improving neighborhoods.
- District scale increases efficiency, but having an infrastructural system at that scale means it needs to be attractive to the public to gain acceptance and become part of its environment.

INNOVATION  9

The burden of infrastructure is often concentrated in communities that do not have the ability to defend against its impacts. The proper allocation of resources and benefits as well as related impacts and their mitigation must be aligned and integrated to the scale of the infrastructural system under consideration. Necessary structures should be put in place to ensure its protection.

Resultant Outcomes for Decision Makers

Equal access to water resources across the demographic spectrum should be the goal. The key idea is about the right to clean water in the context of technology transfer, right sizing innovative systems, community context, and impact mitigation. Pollution concentrates with poverty. The impoverished suffer the most from pollution that they might or might not have created themselves. The Basel Action Network, which champions environmental health and justice, says, "Nobody should choose between poverty and poison." The way we design and redesign our systems should take reversing this as a primary trajectory. Leaders can look for opportunities to bring the rich and poor together through common infrastructural assets. Provision of affordable solutions needs to be aimed at targeting the part of the world where the majority of urban growth is predicted to take place, i.e. the developing world. Infrastructural techniques need to be adapted to the local politics and economic context. Emphasis should be put on diplomatic collaboration, knowledge exchange, and technology transfer.

SOCIAL JUSTICE / ENVIRONMENTAL JUSTICE: COMMUNITY EMPOWERMENT & RESOURCE EQUITY

 Hunts Point Riverside Park was developed in a low-income neighborhood in the Bronx in New York. It was transformed from a derelict dumping site into a neighborhood amenity with access to the waterfront.

INNOVATION  9

Applications of these Innovations Include:

Address power / water pollution injustice and wastewater pollution in poorest neighborhoods

- Distribute costs across demographic sharing in systems function
- Leverage the investments of corporate and academic campuses to enhance a larger vision for the city. Sometimes it takes a brand to carry it out before the city carries it out. Corporate and academic campuses operate at a district scale; transparency of infrastructure as a pedagogical tool speaks to the campus environment.

Democratization of clean water supply

- Preserve/create equal access to critical water resources
- Look for opportunities to clean surface waters
- Engage women of developing countries in the evolution of the infrastructural systems

Restore cohesive and connected ecologies the benefit the full spectrum of the urban population

Prevent contamination of both surface water and groundwater by outdated practices through introduction of innovative design

Learn from local traditions / methods and do not try to implement generic one-size-fits-all solutions.

SOCIAL JUSTICE / ENVIRONMENTAL JUSTICE: COMMUNITY EMPOWERMENT & RESOURCE EQUITY

The location of the Southeast Wastewater Treatment Plant in San Francisco's Bayview-Hunter's Point neighborhood is indicative of a larger trend wherein undesirable land use and pollution lead to negative health impacts among adjacent communities. The environmental justice movement promoting green infrastructure alternatives to grey infrastructure solutions in the United States was born in part out of this site. The community organized to reduce the negative impacts experienced by the treatment plant.

Earth Celebrations Hudson River Pageant is an ecological and social action art project directed by Felicia Young to engage community in restoration efforts of the Hudson River estuary (2009-2012), downtown section of the Hudson River Park, New York City.

The Vaigai River Restoration Pageant & Project is a social action art project to mobilize a local and international collaborative effort to restore the Vaigai River in Madurai, South India.

SOCIAL JUSTICE / ENVIRONMENTAL JUSTICE: COMMUNITY EMPOWERMENT & RESOURCE EQUITY

 Newtown Creek WWTP in Brooklyn, New York was built on one of the most polluted industrial canals in the history of the United States. The Superfund site was cleaned over time. During a recent upgrade of the WWTP, the site was redesigned to include the restoration of a ¼ acre stretch of Newtown Creek Nature Walk that includes public art.

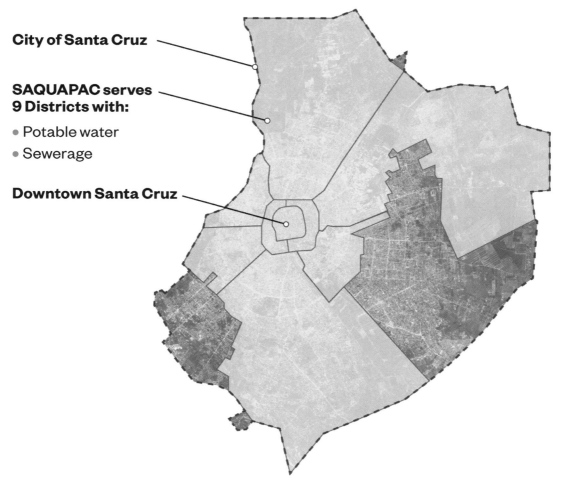

City of Santa Cruz

SAQUAPAC serves 9 Districts with:

- Potable water
- Sewerage

Downtown Santa Cruz

SAGUAPAC is the largest consumer cooperative utility in the world, which formed as a response to corruption within the municipal government in handling water resources. According to the World Bank, SAGUAPAC is one of the best water utilities in Latin America.

Implementation Tips

- Focus on implementation — every design is as good as its implementation.
- Develop regulatory and governance models.
- Address the spatial dynamics of community politics relative to infrastructural investments.
- Address the informal economic sectors where digital technology and telecommunications are flourishing.
- Incentivize developed world to donate/ export only truly operational used e-goods and take responsibility for a regulated disposal of the e-waste.
- Propose a strategy/ vision that would link the mandate of one municipal leader with his/ hers predecessor and the antecessor.

Technology Transfer

This flow is not simply one directional: north to south, south to north. Electronic waste continues to be a pressing issue in today's IT development. Global e-waste sites are presenting a massive environmental, social, and economic burden. More often than properly recycled, e-waste is camouflaged as "still operating goods" and exported to the developing world. Lack of regulation related to disposing of this hazardous waste creates harm to communities who process it.

Imported e-waste mostly ends up in the developing world where workers of the informal sector dismantle it for precious metals or spare parts and burn the rest to minimize the volume and then dump it in the nearby bodies of water. These actions result in the contamination of potable water sources and pose a threat to the human health and the environment. E-waste became a source of livelihood for underprivileged workers of the informal sector. However due to the lack of appropriate facilities, these unsafe procedures simultaneously present a health hazard for both actively exposed workers and passive dwellers of those communities. It is the responsibility of the so-called developed world to take care of the byproducts of its technological advancement in order to provide sustainable solutions.

INNOVATION  10

Urban expansion and development prioritization require planning approaches across jurisdictions to reduce sprawl and address impacts of informal and other developments. Groundwater, surface water, and seawater resources all engage different jurisdictional boundaries and require unique management structures to support equitable access and protection. Broader impact may be achieved by creating a framework for multiple jurisdictions to collaborate than by solely working within a single jurisdiction, in particular when natural boundaries, like watersheds or fresh water supplies, reach across multiple political boundaries. This is an age-old challenge extending from the first human settlements that is now re-exposed to the emerging requirements in governance to address climate risk and technological change.

Climate impacts such as sea level rise, water resources, and watershed stewardship always cross multiple jurisdictions and need a systemic cross-jurisdictional decision-making framework to produce flexibility and equity for citizens.

Resultant Outcomes for Decision Makers

New administrative structures need to be established in order to span the boundaries that reduce system optimization. Formulas and ratios can be developed for the incorporation of bioregional ecology and development of pro-rata allocation for participation to shape localized land reserves, projects, and programs.

MULTI-SCALAR & JURISDICTIONAL FRAMEWORKS FOR COLLABORATION & BIOREGIONAL RESILIENCY

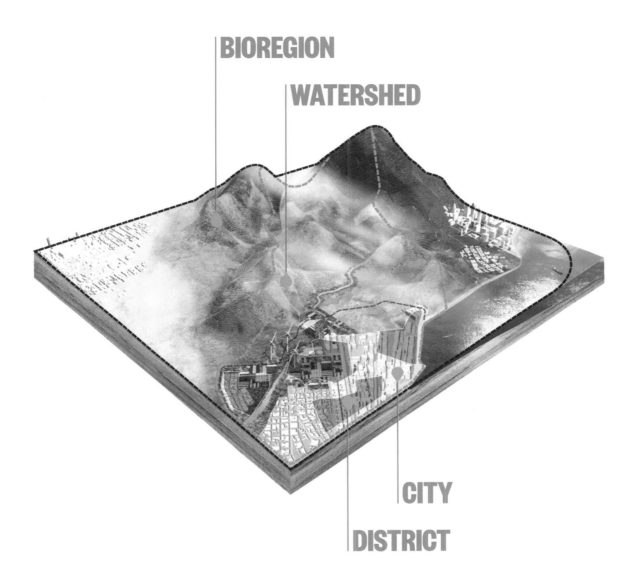

BIOREGION

WATERSHED

CITY

DISTRICT

INNOVATION  10

Applications of these Innovations Include:

Establish regional plans

- There is a need for infrastructure systems to operate in coordination to ensure regional stability, which may include environmental factors and shared resources.
- Create uninterrupted green buffers, greenways, and greenbelts that connect at a bioregional scale (i.e. watershed scale).

Establish urban plans that fit into regional strategy

- Transform urban neighborhood expansion and safe access to public space.

Establish joint powers authority to address regional flooding from SLR agency and municipality cooperation to ensure water and energy resources are properly managed and not compromising one another.

MULTI-SCALAR & JURISDICTIONAL FRAMEWORKS FOR COLLABORATION & BIOREGIONAL RESILIENCY

The Bangalore Lakes Vision Plan was developed as an NGO proposition as a tool to build local consensus around protection of the city's critical and vanishing water resources.

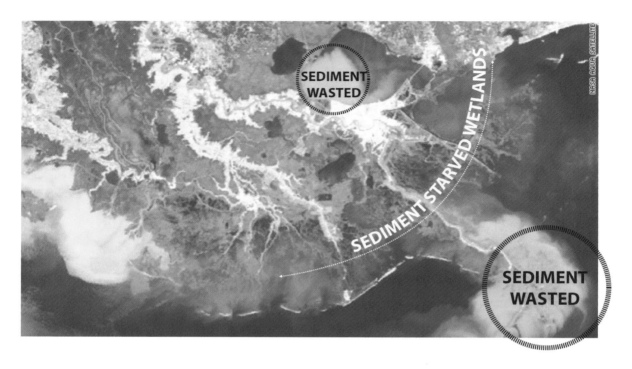

 The Louisiana Coastal Master Plan addresses resiliency planning across multiple jurisdictions to create resilient infrastructure and communities along the Louisiana Gulf Coast. Stakeholders include: government, academia, non-governmental organizations, and citizens.

MULTI-SCALAR & JURISDICTIONAL FRAMEWORKS FOR COLLABORATION & BIOREGIONAL RESILIENCY

Tree planting along Bellandur Lake promotes ecological restoration, water quality, and community engagement. Planting trees restores water-based ecological infrastructure for the city of Bangalore.

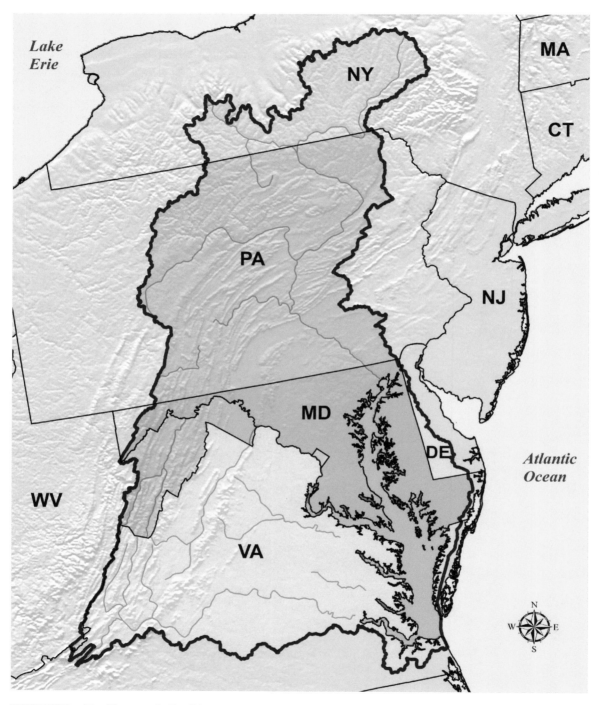

 The Chesapeake Bay Watershed Initiative is one of the most extensive coastal environmental protection programs in the United States. The watershed area crosses multiple state borders pointing to the complexity of aligning natural systems and political boundaries.

MULTI-SCALAR & JURISDICTIONAL FRAMEWORKS FOR COLLABORATION & BIOREGIONAL RESILIENCY

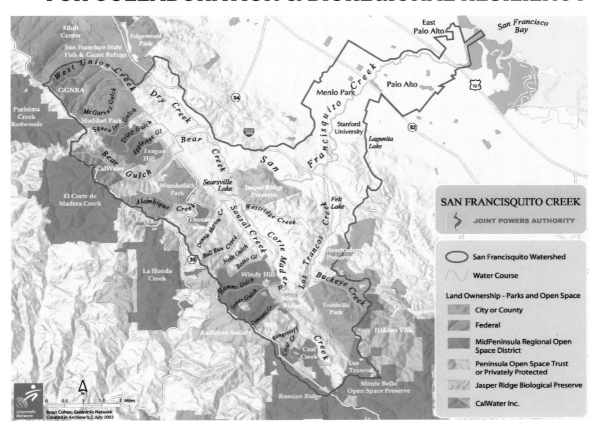

The SFCJPA is an independent regional government agency that leads projects along the San Francisquito Creek and the San Francisco Bay to benefit and connect communities, enhance ecosystems, provide recreational opportunities, and improve regional flood protection.

Implementation Tips

- Mechanisms can be set up for districts to contribute proportional public benefits and receive equitable incentives.

- Tools and strategies need to be in place for aligning science with design and decision making processes.

PART 5

Case Studies

Silicon Valley is a global economic powerhouse. Nevertheless, it is situated in a location vulnerable to both coastal flooding and water shortages. The potential economic impact of flooding and the risk of water shortages can be ameliorated with an integrated systemic design response to provide replicable patterns for resilience for the region. The design proposal suggests several ways to address risks for a more resilient Silicon Valley.

CASE STUDY—SILICON VALLEY

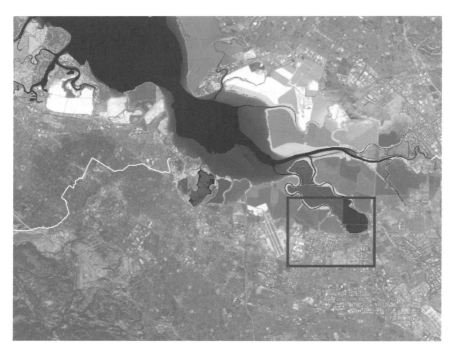

CURRENT SEA LEVEL

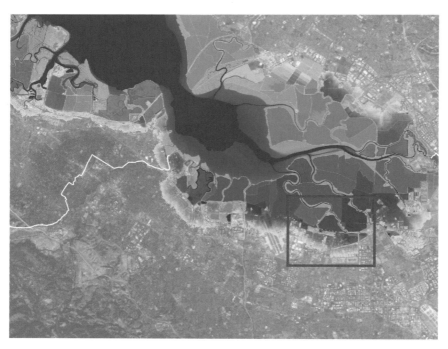

1.2 METERS (4 FEET) SEA LEVEL RISE

According to Save the Bay, "more than $60 billion in homes, businesses, and crucial infrastructure is at risk" of severe flooding due to extreme weather and rising sea levels in the Bay Area.

0.6 METERS (2 FEET) SEA LEVEL RISE

1.8 METERS (6 FEET) SEA LEVEL RISE

The site consists of office parks, a wastewater treatment plant, sports field and a park, ponds, and tidal marsh. Low-income housing is located south of the major highway crossing through the site. A rethinking of the land use can be a tool for resiliency planning.

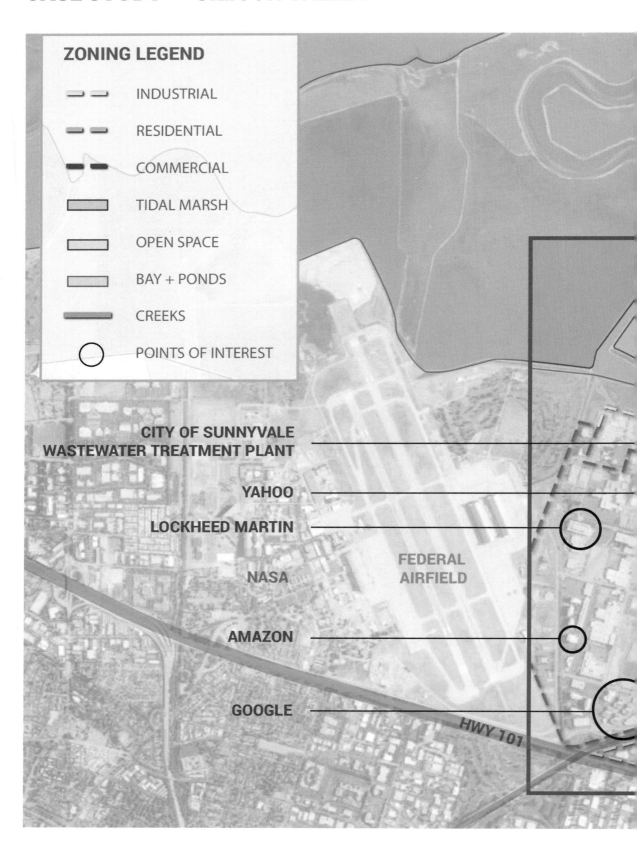

ZONING LEGEND

- — — INDUSTRIAL
- — — RESIDENTIAL
- — — COMMERCIAL
- TIDAL MARSH
- OPEN SPACE
- BAY + PONDS
- CREEKS
- ◯ POINTS OF INTEREST

CITY OF SUNNYVALE WASTEWATER TREATMENT PLANT

YAHOO

LOCKHEED MARTIN

NASA

FEDERAL AIRFIELD

AMAZON

GOOGLE

HWY 101

TIDAL
MARSH

HWY

CASE STUDY—SILICON VALLEY

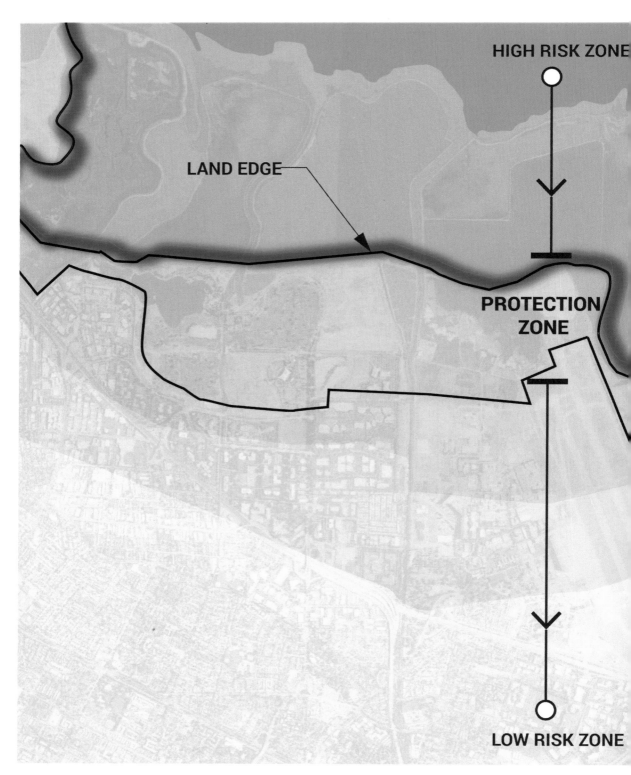

Looking at the site in relation to how sea level rise will affect development, there is a distinct opportunity to protect critical infrastructure within the urbanized coastal edge historically used for infrastructure and recreation.

CASE STUDY—SILICON VALLEY

1st Layer

2

Landscape is used to create layers of protection for critical infrastructure and development.
Districts share resources through water, energy, and waste management infrastructure to provide
locally produced water, energy, and fertilizers.

LEGEND

CREEKS
DISTRICTS
WASTEWATER TREATMENT PLANT
LIVING BERM
AREA OF CRITICAL RISK
HORIZONTAL LEVEE
TIDAL GATES
CENTRAL UTILITY PLANT
STORMWATER PARK
CONNECTION: WATER + DATA

2nd Layer of Protection

3rd Layer of Protection

CASE STUDY—SILICON VALLEY

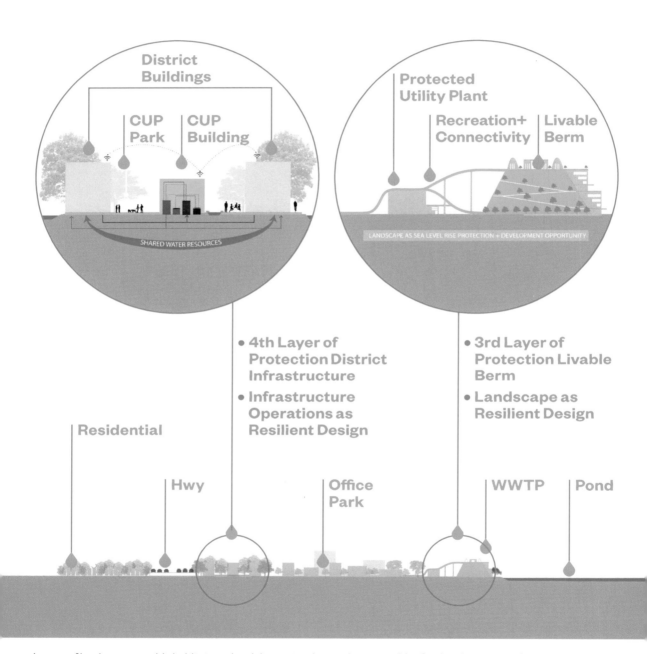

District Buildings

CUP Park **CUP Building**

SHARED WATER RESOURCES

Protected Utility Plant

Recreation+ Connectivity **Livable Berm**

LANDSCAPE AS SEA LEVEL RISE PROTECTION + DEVELOPMENT OPPORTUNITY

- 4th Layer of Protection District Infrastructure
- Infrastructure Operations as Resilient Design

- 3rd Layer of Protection Livable Berm
- Landscape as Resilient Design

Residential

Hwy

Office Park

WWTP **Pond**

Layers of landscape provide habitat, sea level rise protection, and opportunities for development and recreation to create a more resilient site socially, ecologically, and economically.

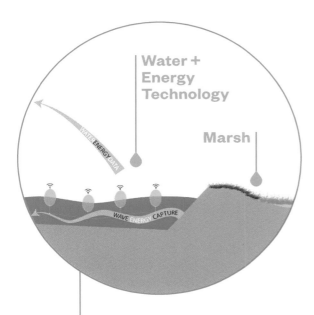

**Water +
Energy
Technology**

Marsh

WATER ENERGY DATA

WAVE ENERGY CAPTURE

- **Water + Energy
  Technology**
- **Landscape as
  Energy Producer**

- **2nd Layer
  of Protection
  Marsh**
- **Landscape
  as Resilient
  Design**

- **1st Layer of
  Protection
  Horizontal Levee**
- **Landscape as
  Redilient Design**

Bay

CASE STUDY—BANGALORE

The water situation in Bangalore is dire. In fact the city may even face the risk of water scarcity-forced evacuations within the next ten years. Lack of access to clean water is a major issue at this site because of the severe environmental degradation of Bellandur Lake and the surrounding network of waterways. Bellandur Lake is a source of drinking water for residents adjacent to the lake who do not have other access to drinking water. The design proposal suggests several ways to address the current threat to water quality and vulnerable residents.

Bellandur Lake is extremely polluted by domestic and industrial wastewater. Foam from industrial contaminants pollutes drinking water and even catches fire periodically.

CASE STUDY—BANGALORE

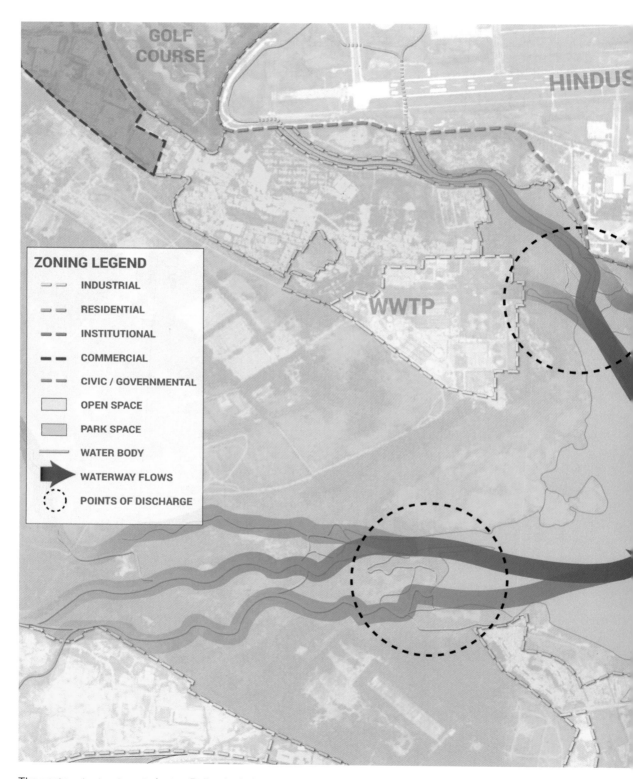

ZONING LEGEND

- – – INDUSTRIAL
- – – RESIDENTIAL
- – – INSTITUTIONAL
- – – COMMERCIAL
- – – CIVIC / GOVERNMENTAL
- OPEN SPACE
- PARK SPACE
- — WATER BODY
- WATERWAY FLOWS
- POINTS OF DISCHARGE

GOLF COURSE

HINDUS

WWTP

The wastewater treatment plant on Bellandur Lake discharges partially treated water. Nutrients in the water contribute to damaged human and ecological health.

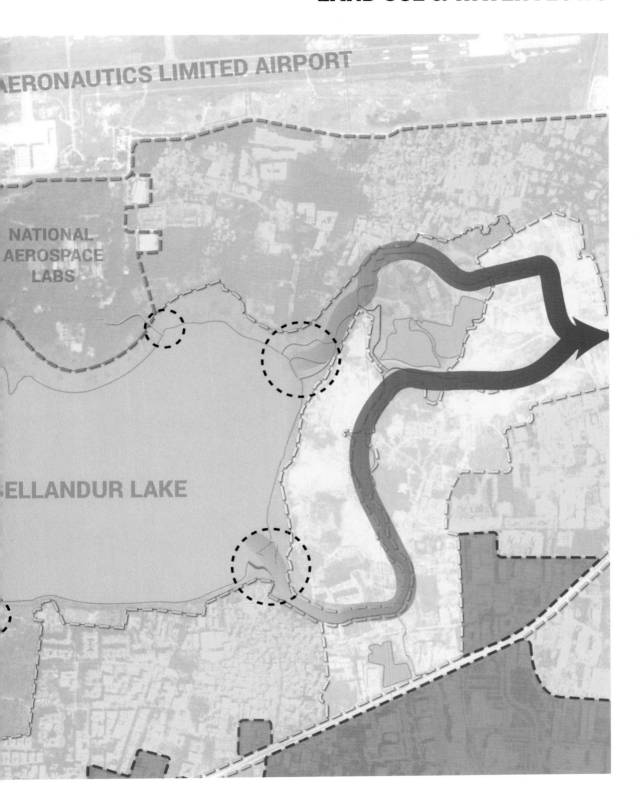

AERONAUTICS LIMITED AIRPORT

NATIONAL
AEROSPACE
LABS

ELLANDUR LAKE

CASE STUDY—BANGALORE

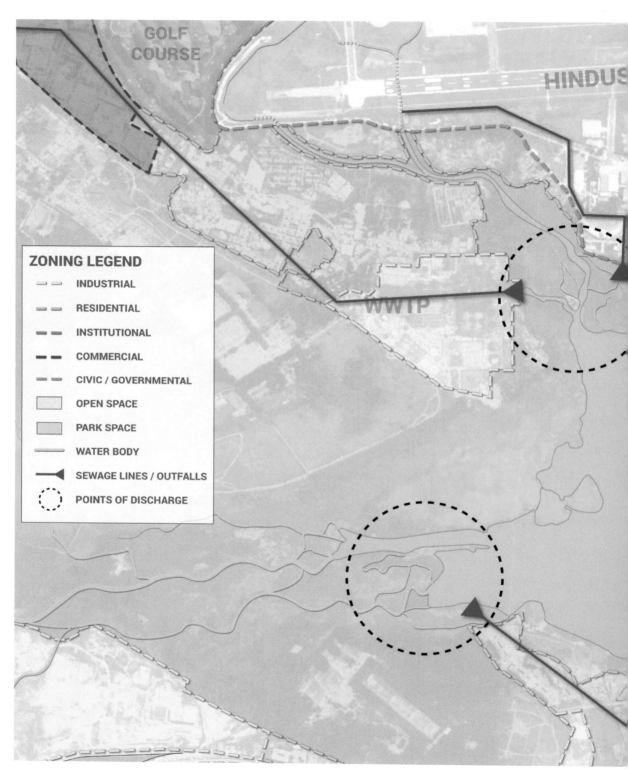

ZONING LEGEND

- – – **INDUSTRIAL**
- – – **RESIDENTIAL**
- – – **INSTITUTIONAL**
- – – **COMMERCIAL**
- – – **CIVIC / GOVERNMENTAL**
- **OPEN SPACE**
- **PARK SPACE**
- **WATER BODY**
- **SEWAGE LINES / OUTFALLS**
- **POINTS OF DISCHARGE**

GOLF COURSE

HINDUS

WWTP

Residential and industrial waste enter the lake at four main points. These points of pollution are also points of opportunity for resource recovery and value creation.

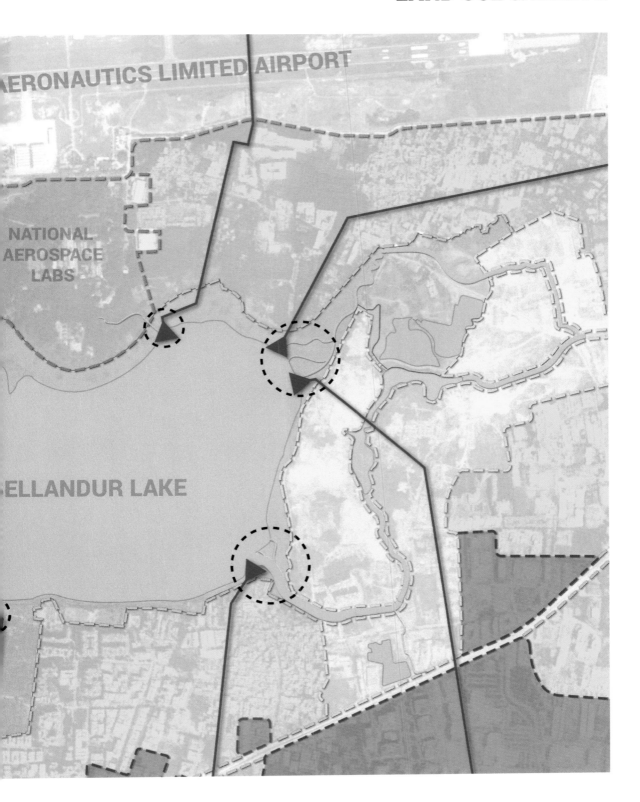

AERONAUTICS LIMITED AIRPORT

NATIONAL
AEROSPACE
LABS

BELLANDUR LAKE

CASE STUDY—BANGALORE

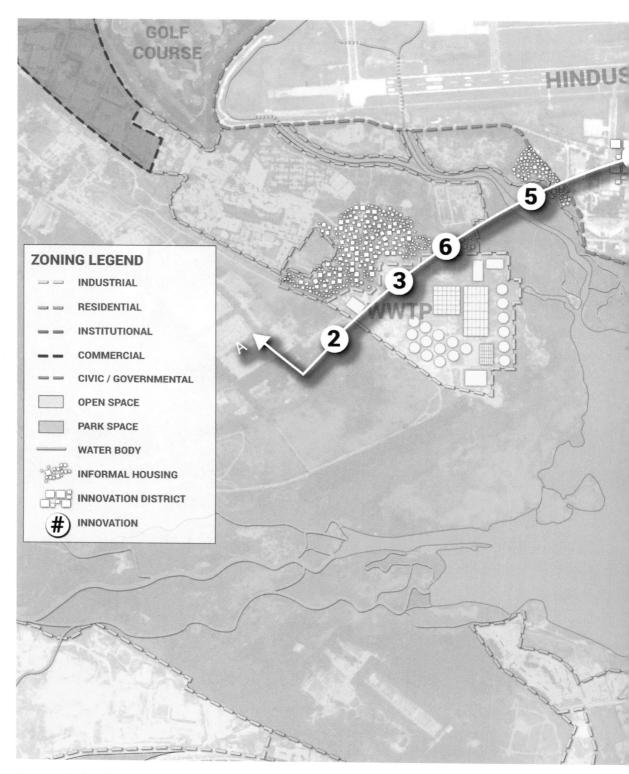

Proposed design elements address wastewater pollution and the need for slums to have necessary infrastructure for improved habitability.

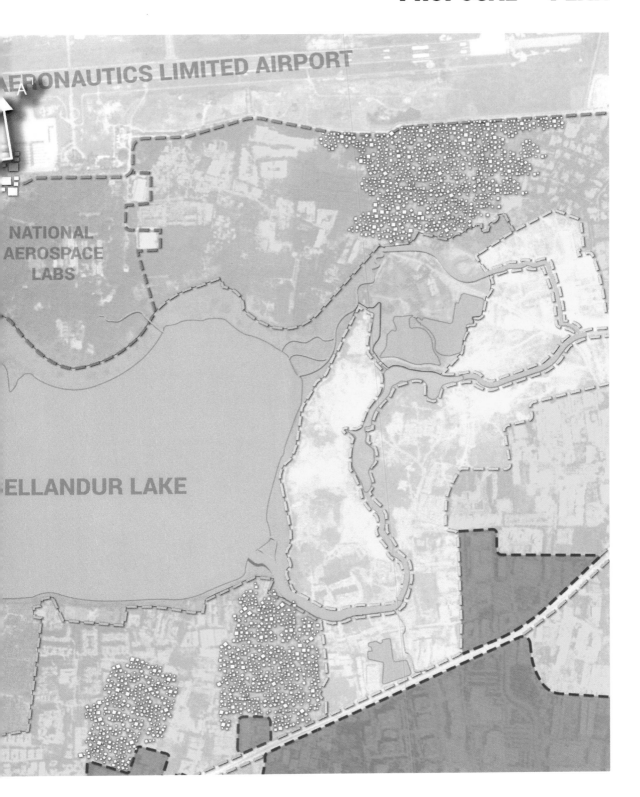

AERONAUTICS LIMITED AIRPORT

NATIONAL
AEROSPACE
LABS

BELLANDUR LAKE

CASE STUDY—BANGALORE

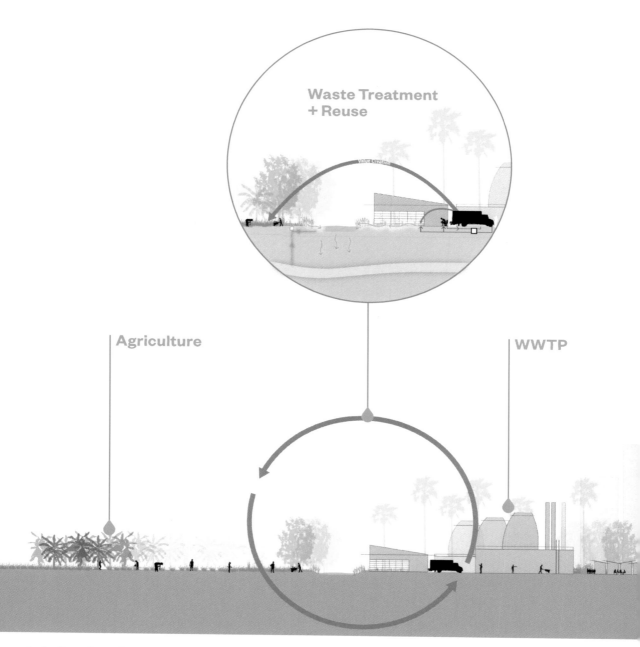

Waste Treatment + Reuse

Agriculture

WWTP

Agriculture plots adjacent to the wastewater treatment plant can share resources. Bolt-on systems can adapt treatment plants and provide economic opportunities. A riparian buffer next to the stream (nala) improves water quality and provides recreational amenities. Ecological restoration and improved wastewater infrastructure is critical to provide habitable communities for the people living around Bellandur Lake.

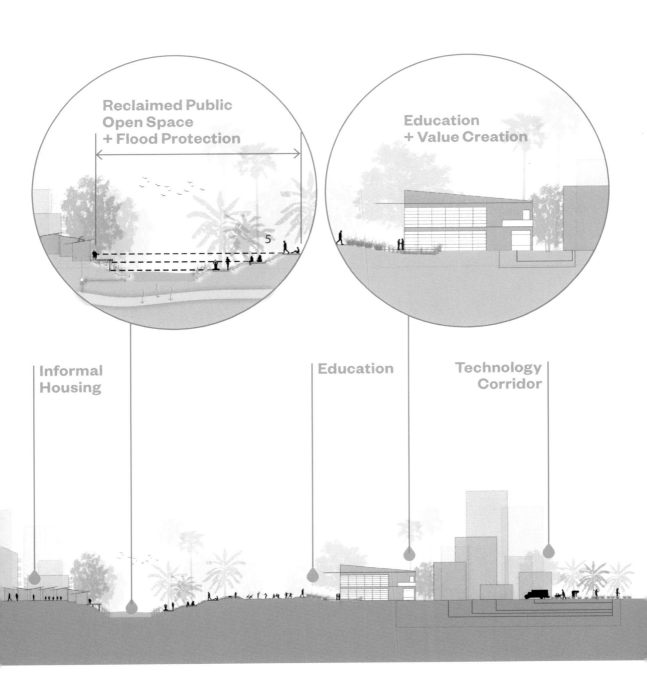

Reclaimed Public Open Space + Flood Protection

Education + Value Creation

Informal Housing

Education

Technology Corridor

Water,
Finite Res
Precious
We Need 1
Attentive.

ource.

Resource.

o Be

CONCLUSION

The innovations presented here are meant to provide a meaningful contribution to the tremendous task at hand for cities dealing with the emerging and comprehensive challenges related to water, flooding, and sanitation. These recommendations have been put forward with the hope that some portion of the trillions of dollars being invested in urban expansion and its infrastructure can be steered to support equitable, multi-functional, and resilient systems embedded in public space that improve people's connections to their cities and to each other.

Implementation of the innovative and decentralized strategies listed and tested in this publication will help municipal and national leaders in both the developed and developing world address systemic risks. The United Nations New Urban Agenda clearly states the need for ensuring the equitable access to physical and social infrastructure; this publication provides a response to that request. In order to carry these ideas forward, we will need the next generation of urban designers, planners, academics, engineers, and policy-makers to get involved and build public awareness. Infrastructure is a critical component of urban design and one that must be addressed to enable healthy and inclusive urban growth that serves all citizens.

ENDNOTES

1   Capelli, Kara and Howard Perlman, "How Much Water is Available," USGS. May 2012. Accessed February 2016.
http://www.usgs.gov/blogs/features/usgs_top_story/how-much-water-is-available/

2   World Bank, Climate Risks and Adaptation in Asian Coastal Megacities: A Synthesis Report, "Assessing Damage Costs and Prioritizing Adaptation Options," 2010.
http://documents.worldbank.org/curated/en/2010/09/12886839/climate-risks-adaptation-asian-coastal-megacities-synthesis-report

3   Wood, James, "Province boosts cost of Alberta floods to $6 billion," Calgary Herald. September 23, 2013. Accessed February 2016.
http://www.calgaryherald.com/news/Province+boosts+cost+Alberta+floods+-billion/8952392/story.html

4   Hallegatte, Stephane, et al, "Future flood losses in major coastal cities," Nature, p. 802-806. August 2013. Accessed February 2016.
http://www.nature.com/nclimate/journal/v3/n9/full/nclimate1979.html

5   EPA, "Water Audits and Water Loss Control for Public Water Systems," July 2013.

6   Corcoran, E., C. Nellemann, E. Baker, R. Bos, D. Osborn, H. Savelli (eds). 2010. Sick Water? The central role of waste- water management in sustainable development. A Rapid Re- sponse Assessment. United Nations Environment Pro- gramme, UN-HABITAT, GRID-Arendal.
www.grida.no

7   Baldé, C.P., Wang, F., Kuehr, R., Huisman, J. (2015), The global e-waste monitor – 2014, United Nations University, IAS – SCYCLE, Bonn, Germany.

8   United Nations, Department of Economic and Social Affairs, Population Division (2014). World Urbanization Prospects: The 2014 Revision, Highlights (ST/ESA/SER.A/352).

9   Seto, Karen, Burak Guneralp, and Lucy Hutyra, "Global forecasts of urban expansion to 2030 and direct impacts on biodiversity and carbon pools," PNAS, Arizona State University, Aug 16, 2012.

10   United Nations, Department of Economic and Social Affairs, Population Division (2014). World Urbanization Prospects: The 2014 Revision, Highlights (ST/ESA/SER.A/352).

11   Ibid.

12   United Nations, Department of Economic and Social Affairs, Population Division (2015). World Population Prospects: The 2015 Revision, Key Findings and Advance Tables. Working Paper No. ESA/P/WP.241.

13   United Nations, Department of Economic and Social Affairs, Population Division (2014). World Urbanization Prospects: The 2014 Revision, Highlights (ST/ESA/SER.A/352).

14   McKinsey & Company, "Infrastructure productivity: How to save $1 trillion a year," January 2013.

15   Corcoran, E., C. Nellemann, E. Baker, R. Bos, D. Osborn, H. Savelli (eds). 2010. Sick Water? The central role of waste- water management in sustainable development. A Rapid Re- sponse Assessment. United Nations Environment Pro- gramme, UN-HABITAT, GRID-Arendal.
www.grida.no

16   McKinsey & Company, "Infrastructure productivity: How to save $1 trillion a year," January 2013.

IMAGE CREDITS

Special thanks to Sherwood Design Engineers for images
and diagrams throughout this text

Water Infrastructure: Equitable Development of Resilient Systems
Ed. S. Bry Sarté and Morana M. Stipisic

Urban Innovation
Series curated by Kate Orff
Director of the Urban Design program

Published by
Columbia University
Graduate School of Architecture, Planning, and Preservation (GSAPP)
407 Avery Hall, 1172 Amsterdam Avenue
New York, NY 10027

Visit our website at www.arch.columbia.edu/books

This book has been produced through the Office of the Dean, Amale Andraos, and the Office of Publications.

Production Coordination: Caitlin Blanchfield
Graphic Design: Manuel Miranda Studio

978-1-941332-26-9

CPSIA information can be obtained at www.ICGtesting.com
Printed in the USA
BVIW12n0021300916
462957BV00009B/5